Running to Extremes

DEDICATION

To the enduring legacy and memory of Ted Corbitt

SCOTT LUDWIG
WITH
BONNIE BUSCH, CRAIG SNAPP, MARSHA WHITE,
DAVID CORFMAN & NORM KLEIN

RUNNING TO EXTREMES

THE LEGENDARY ATHLETES OF ULTRARUNNING

Meyer & Meyer Sport

British Library Cataloguing in Publication Data
A catalogue record for this book is available from the British Library

Running to Extremes
Maidenhead: Meyer & Meyer Sport (UK) Ltd., 2016
ISBN: 978-1-78255-080-8

All rights reserved. Except for use in a review, no part of this publication may be reproduced, stored in a retrieval system, or transmitted, in any form or by any means now known or here-after invented without the prior written permission of the publisher.
This book may not be lent, resold, hired out or otherwise disposed of by way of trade in any form, binding or cover other than that which is published, without the prior written consent of the publisher.

© 2016 by Meyer & Meyer Sport (UK) Ltd.
Aachen, Auckland, Beirut, Cairo, Cape Town, Dubai, Hägendorf, Hong Kong,
Indianapolis, Manila, New Delhi, Singapore, Sydney, Tehran, Vienna
 Member of the World Sport Publishers' Association (WSPA)
Manufacturing: Versa Press inc., Il, USA
ISBN: 978-1-78255-080-8
E-Mail: info@m-m-sports.com
www.m-m-sports.com

TABLE OF CONTENTS

DEDICATION 2

HERE'S WHAT OTHERS HAVE TO SAY ABOUT
RUNNING TO EXTREMES 8

INTRODUCTION 11

THE FATHER OF LONG DISTANCE RUNNING 15

THREE THINGS YOU NEED TO KNOW
(BEFORE READING THIS BOOK) 21

FOREWORD BY GARY CORBITT 22

CHAPTER 1 **RAY ZAHAB** 26

CHAPTER 2 **MIKE SMITH** 42

CHAPTER 3 **AMY PALMIERO-WINTERS** 52

CHAPTER 4 **DEAN KARNAZES** 70

CHAPTER 5 **MARK COVERT** 82

CHAPTER 6 **BOBBI GIBB** 98

CHAPTER 7 **MIKE MORTON** 108

RUNNING TO EXTREMES

CHAPTER 8 **MARSHALL ULRICH** 118

CHAPTER 9 **PAM REED** 128

CHAPTER 11 **LARRY MACON** 138

CHAPTER 12 **TIM TWIETMEYER** 154

CHAPTER 12 **HELEN KLEIN** 164

CHAPTER 13 **ERIC CLIFTON** 174

CHAPTER 14 **ED ETTINGHAUSEN** 186

CHAPTER 15 **ANN TRASON** 202

AUTHORS AND CONTRIBUTORS 218

EPILOGUE 226

ACKNOWLEDGEMENTS 229

APPENDICES 231

CREDITS 259

TABLE OF CONTENTS

RUNNING TO **EXTREMES**

HERE'S WHAT OTHERS HAVE TO SAY ABOUT RUNNING TO EXTREMES

> *"I believe all of us are born to be explorers, and those who discover this are the luckiest people of all. Distance runners certainly fall into this category. Those who truly love life and the world they live in chase after life with every bit of gusto they have, and that transforms them into extreme runners. I truly enjoyed reading Running to Extremes."*
>
> -Bill Rodgers, four-time winner of both the Boston Marathon and New York City Marathon

> *"Ted Corbitt always stood for me as a symbol of how through large efforts (such as his pioneering work in course certification and his selfless volunteering) and little gestures (he once surprised me with a cake at the end of a race), someone can advance a sport and touch people's lives. I welcome this book that recognizes his achievements by highlighting Ted and some of those who followed in his footsteps."*
>
> -Ann Trason, 14-time winner of the Western States Endurance Run

TABLE OF CONTENTS

"I am honored to be included with such an amazing list of athletes and people in Scott Ludwig's book. Through their passion for living life to the fullest, these are the people who inspire me; I hope they do the same for you."

-Marshall Ulrich, extreme endurance athlete and author of *Running on Empty: An Ultramarathoner's Story of Love, Loss, and a Record-Setting Run Across America*

"Scott and his team of writers have compiled an outstanding collection of the most prolific endurance athletes in the world. I'm excited to be included and hope this book proves to others that what appears to be impossible is indeed possible."

-Ray Zahab, one of only three men to have run across the Sahara Desert

"This book does an excellent job of honoring Ted Corbitt and the other founding fathers of long-distance running. Running to Extremes will be an important part of the running history continuum for generations of participants, fans, historians, and scholars."

-Gary Corbitt, curator of the Ted Corbitt Archives

RUNNING TO EXTREMES

"I am so grateful I still love to run. I encourage people to step outside the box and do something different to mix things up; it keeps it exciting. Keep putting one foot in front of the other and never stop."

-Pam Reed, two-time winner of the Badwater Ultramarathon

'Trail and ultrarunning have created a never-ending source of new challenges as well as friendships and experiences that road racing just can't provide."

–Mike Smith, trail and ultrarunner

INTRODUCTION

Early in 2012, my friend and accomplished ultrarunner, Amy Costa, invited me to participate in a conference call. Ordinarily I make it a practice to stay as far away from conference calls as possible for a variety of reasons: poor connections, trying to listen to more than one person speak at the same time, not always knowing who is speaking, people speaking just to hear themselves talk, and wondering if someone is on the call who hasn't been announced as *being* on the call. Man, I avoid conference calls like I do the bubonic plague and chick flicks.

But not this one.

This conference call was different. This call was being hosted by Gary Corbitt, son of the late Ted Corbitt. You may recognize Ted Corbitt as the father of long-distance running. Ted Corbitt was one of the first distance runners who inspired me to become a distance runner. He was among the inaugural class of inductees into the National Distance Running Hall of Fame (1998) as well as the inaugural class of inductees into the American Ultrarunning Hall of Fame (2006). The purpose of the call was to preserve the history of road running, and the call was going to be recorded. For the first time in my life I was actually excited about being on a conference call. Actually, *giddy* might be a better word.

The participants on the call included a veritable who's who in the world of distance running:

- Park Barner, former U.S. and world record holder in the 24-hour run
- Fritz Mueller, who, at age 42, ran a 2:20:47 Boston Marathon and, in 1978, won the World Masters Marathon Championship in Berlin

RUNNING TO EXTREMES

- Rob Deines and John Garlepp, former 50-mile U.S. record holders; Garlepp was a former running rival of Ted Corbitt and the current coach of the renowned Millrose Athletic Association
- Rich Benyo, established ultrarunner and editor of *Marathon & Beyond*
- Ray Krolewicz, former U.S. record holder in the 48-hour run and finisher of over 400 ultramarathons
- Phil McCarthy, current U.S. record holder in the 48-hour run
- Neil Weygandt, finisher of the last 45 Boston Marathons
- Jacqueline Hansen, 1973 and 1975 Boston Marathon winner and two-time world record holder in the women's marathon
- John Chodes, author of a biography on Ted Corbitt

Gary started the call by reading a letter from Bruce Fordyce, nine-time winner of the Comrades Marathon. Gary then introduced a true ultrarunning legend, Bernard Gomersall, winner of the 1965 Comrades Marathon and four-time winner (1963-1966) of the London-to-Brighton road race.

Bernard reminisced about his battles on the road with the ultrarunners of the 1960s, including his thrilling one-minute victory over Ted Corbitt at London-to-Brighton in 1964. His stories were so vivid it was as if they had taken place yesterday. Asked if he continues to run, Bernard stated he has arthritis in both knees and at the advice (nay, *insistence*) of his doctor is not allowed to run anymore. He remains active in a variety of other non-contact sports but misses the days when running 75 to 80 miles a week (and up to 110 miles a week leading up to important competitions) was the norm. Soon Bernard, a widower, announced he would be leaving his native England and moving to Maryland so that he can be close to his daughter.

INTRODUCTION

The call was then opened up to others, and the topics were many:

- The first AAU National 50-Mile Championship (Staten Island, New York) in 1966 when the temperature reached an almost intolerable 85 degrees Fahrenheit. The winner was Jim McDonagh in 5:52:28.
- Ted Corbitt's goal in the 1966 60-Mile Championship race: to hit the marathon mark in a brisk 2:42, only to be disappointed when his 26.2-mile split was 2:49.
- The days when running competitions of significant distance had drinking regulations; in other words, no drinking prior to the 10-kilometer mark. (One person commented they saw runners disqualified for breaking this rule.)
- Competitions that included actor and accomplished (in his own right) ultrarunner, Bruce Dern.
- Park Barner, in his humble and soft-spoken manner, noting he now runs an average of two miles a day as he has a shoulder that "doesn't agree" with his running (while not mentioning he at one time held the U.S. record in the 24-hour run with 152-plus miles, which bettered the former record by over 16 miles and later held the world record with 161 miles). Note: He did mention, however, that he loves to bowl and manages to maintain a 200 average. (Note to this note: In my opinion, a 200 bowling average is bowling's equivalent of running 152 miles in 24 hours.)

Amy and I were both as quiet as dormice during the call, content on intently listening to the legends relive a time that was essentially the birth of ultrarunning.

In our own way, we were able to relive history, and we were very grateful for every second—and every *mile*—of it.

RUNNING TO EXTREMES

Those 105 minutes on that call inspired me to do my part in preserving the legacy of ultrarunning for generations to come. I couldn't think of a better way than to write about those whose lives have been inspired by those who have run countless miles before them.

I hope you enjoy reading about them.

–Scott Ludwig

Marshall Ulrich and Scott Ludwig, Evergreen, Colorado, July 2015

THE FATHER OF LONG DISTANCE RUNNING

I have my doubts as to whether or not I would have ever considered running an ultra if it weren't for the influence, nay the *legend,* of Ted Corbitt.

Ted Corbitt is known not only in running circles but also around the globe as the father of American ultrarunning. Born in 1919, it would be 31 years before Corbitt would begin training to run marathons. He was virtually an instant success, earning a spot on the 1952 U.S. Olympic marathon team. Four years later he would miss qualifying for the team by only one spot.

Ted Corbitt and Ann Trason

RUNNING TO **EXTREMES**

Corbitt was born during a period when racial discrimination was prevalent. While his classmates would ride the bus to school, young Corbitt opted to walk; it was during these treks to and from school that he would discover how much he enjoyed running.

Competing as a track athlete in high school, Corbitt learned about the exploits of Tarzan Brown, a Narragansett Indian who won the Boston Marathon in 1936 and again in 1939. Corbitt was intrigued to discover that people could run 26.2 miles. At that time, four miles was considered a long distance to run; marathons did not have the national recognition they have today.

Corbitt attended the University of Cincinnati where he competed in distances ranging from sprints to the two-mile run. He excelled at every distance and would graduate with honors while earning a degree in physical education.

Corbitt took a brief hiatus from his diligent training program when he served in the army during World War II, got married, held a steady job, and earned a master's degree in physical therapy from New York University (1950). It was then he remembered his high school promise to himself of one day running the Boston Marathon—just to see if he could.

In 1951, Corbitt proved to himself that he could, finishing 15th at the most prestigious marathon in the world with a time of 2:48:42. For an encore he ran two more marathons over the next two months in comparable times before qualifying for the Olympic marathon team the following year.

In 1959, Corbitt participated in one of the first modern American ultras, the New York Road Runner Club's 30-miler. Fittingly, he won in a time of 3:04:13, and the event kick-started the sport in the United States. Over the next six years, Corbitt finished first in his first 17 ultramarathons in the U.S.

While maintaining a job as a physical therapist at the International Center for the Disabled, being a husband, raising a son, and working on running-related administrative duties during the night, Corbitt maintained a diligent and hard-to-fathom training regimen. He would run two, sometimes three, times a day. He would run around the entire island of Manhattan (31 miles) not once but oftentimes twice. His weekly mileage would fall in the range of 200 to 300 miles, his monthly mileage exceeding 800 miles—occasionally as much as 1,000 miles or more.

In 1962, Corbitt made his first appearance at the 52.7-mile London-to-Brighton road race in England. Corbitt was among the leaders in the first half of the race before ultimately finishing in fourth, a performance noted by Andy Milroy as signaling the rebirth of North American ultrarunning. Corbitt would return to England four more times to run the event, finishing second on three occasions, including a one-minute loss in 1964 to the number-one ranked ultrarunner in the world at the time, Bernard Gomersall. The race is considered one of the epic, classic duels in the history of the sport.

Ted Corbitt was not only a pioneer athlete in the world of running, but he was also at the forefront as an advocate in the world of running. He was the third president of the Road Runners Club of America (RRCA) and was elected to be the first president of the New York Road Runners Club in 1958. Corbitt helped launch the promotion of a national ultrarunning program by the Amateur Athletic Union (AAU) and RRCA, resulting in the inaugural AAU National 50-Mile Championship in 1966. Corbitt finished second in the first edition of the event (Jim McDonagh was the winner), but he would return to win the championship in 1968, running 50 miles in 5:39:45. He authored and published the booklet,

RUNNING TO EXTREMES

Measuring Road Running Courses, in August of 1964. This document initiated a program for accurate course measurement in the United States. This ensured the legitimacy of the sport of long-distance running with verifiable record keeping.

Corbitt was one of the early proponents of the masters division for runners 40 years of age or older. One of his proudest accomplishments was the development of the standards for course measurement — standards that are now followed by the many USATF-certified races throughout the country. It was Corbitt's desire to make running a truly legitimate sport. By providing runners with accurate courses to compete, they could establish verified times and records to establish standards recognized around the world.

Ted Corbitt was one of the five inductees in the inaugural class of the National Distance Running Hall of Fame in 1998. The other four inductees were Bill Rodgers, Frank Shorter, Joan Samuelson, and Kathrine Switzer. In 2006, Corbitt was inducted into the American Ultrarunning Hall of Fame.

Corbitt dropped out of serious competition in 1974 because of bronchial asthma. At the time he was training for an attempt at bettering the record for running across the United States. (Corbitt felt he was capable of running the 2,800 miles from Los Angeles to New York in 42 days.) In spite of his health problems, Corbitt continued to run simply because he loved it. Although running became more of a physical challenge in his later years, Corbitt continued to participate (primarily walking) in marathons, 100-milers, and several 24-hour races. At the age of 82, he completed 303 miles in a six-day event — just for fun, as well as to achieve a goal and as a personal challenge.

Ted Corbitt, at the age of 88, died on December 12, 2007, in Houston, Texas. Suffering from prostate and colon cancer, Corbitt ultimately died of respiratory failure.

Ted Corbitt's philosophy on running was a simple one. He was quoted in *First Marathons: Personal Encounters With the 26.2-Mile Monster* as saying:

> *You don't need a goal.*
>
> *You don't need a race.*
>
> *You don't need the hype of a so-called fitness craze.*
>
> *All you need is a cheap pair of shoes and some time.*
>
> *The rest will follow.*

Ted Corbitt's wife, Ruth, died in 1989. He is survived by his son, Gary Corbitt of Jacksonville, Florida.

Gary has launched a site on Facebook, **Ted Corbitt – Pioneer,** and a website dedicated to his father at **www.tedcorbitt.com.** His goal is to not only recognize his father, but also to pay tribute to the many pioneers in running and health rehabilitation fields. Please take some time to visit these websites.

I have grown to know Gary through email and telephone correspondence over the past couple of years. When I presented the idea for this book to him and asked if he would be willing to share his father's story, he agreed. For that we can all be grateful because it's highly doubtful that the people portrayed in this book would have ever accomplished the things they have without Ted Corbitt's influence, efforts, and sacrifices. As you will soon find out, Gary also generously agreed to write the foreword to this book.

Gary, thank you for allowing me to share your father's story. I'm certain runners everywhere join me in my sentiments.

Scott Ludwig

Senoia, Georgia

THREE THINGS YOU NEED TO KNOW (BEFORE READING THIS BOOK)

1. All of the information, quotes, and material for this book are based on personal communications—primarily telephone conversations and correspondence through electronic mail—between the authors and their respective subjects. The exception is the chapter on Helen Klein, written by her husband Norm.

2. The athletes portrayed in this book are what I refer to as 'moving targets.' As the majority of the book was written by mid-2015 to meet publishing deadlines, it is highly probable that by the time you are reading this these athletes will have added to their impressive resumes.

3. Don't be intimidated by their accomplishments. Rather, be inspired.

-Scott Ludwig

RUNNING TO EXTREMES

FOREWORD BY GARY CORBITT

Running to Extremes is a fitting tribute to my father, Ted Corbitt, and his legendary and pioneering work in long-distance running. Scott Ludwig has assembled a team of writers and contributors who tell some quite amazing stories about a number of history's most prolific ultrarunners. Scott is an ambassador to the sport of running through his books and as president of the Darkside Running Club. His message as president of the club states "if you're a runner looking for inspiration…motivation…that little something extra to keep you focused and connected to the greatest sport on the planet—RUNNING—you've come to the right place." The same can be said about this, his latest book.

Growing up, I had a unique experience watching the sport of running being invented. I'd like to take this opportunity to review the early eras of ultrarunning and name some of the pioneers in this sport.

The sport has certainly evolved. During the 1960s and early 1970s Ted Corbitt had only one opportunity to run a 100-mile and 24-hour race. Both efforts resulted in American records, but each race turned out to be off days for what he was capable of doing, both in time and distance. I'm still amazed after reading this manuscript to learn about Iron Mike's goal of competing in one hundred 100-mile races in his career, Ed Ettinghausen's completion of 40 races of 100 miles or longer in a single calendar year, and Mark Covert's incredible career longevity.

One of the first extraordinary tests of endurance occurred in 1809 when Captain Robert Barclay, a Scottish aristocrat, walked 1,000 miles in 1,000 successive hours (nearly six weeks) at Newmarket in the United Kingdom. Barclay is also credited with competing in the first 24-hour race in October 1806.

FOREWORD BY GARY CORBITT

My father would talk about his desire to run 600 miles in six days and walk 100 miles in less than 24 hours. I didn't understand the significance of these pedestrian-era performances until after his passing. The pedestrian era (1870s) was when the sport of ultrarunning and walking began to flourish. At the time this was America's favorite spectator sport until interest started to grow in baseball, boxing, and cycling in the 1890s. The events were held in big arenas—like New York's Madison Square Garden—and included big prize purses, huge crowds, circus-like sideshows, lots of betting, and alcohol. Bands and even orchestras were employed by the promoters to entertain both the crowd and the men on the track. The prize money made these athletes wealthy. Frank Hart, the first African American running world record holder earned $21,567, or the equivalent of $480,000 today, in a six-day race. Edward Payson Weston was responsible for the birth of the professional pedestrian era. He was the first to cover 500 miles by foot in six days in 1874. A pedestrian rule change in the late 1870s took the go-as-you-please, or walking, matches into both walking and running. As the sport grew in popularity with the public, it naturally also grew in popularity with the gamblers. This led to its downfall as rumors of fixing matches became widespread.

I was moved in reading the chapter on Mark Covert. His 45-year streak of consecutive days of running started on July 22, 1968. The date was within days of when my father's 13 years of consecutive two runs per day ended. On July 24, 1968, Ted Corbitt ran his signature morning 20-mile workout to work. He ran 3 miles at lunch and another 13 miles home. He was within three miles of home on his evening run when he was injured from an encounter with a dog. All endeavors, occupations, and sports have a history and lineage. Records are set and broken; streaks are started and ended. The ultrarunning streak baton was passed from Ted to Mark in July 1968.

The sport of ultrarunning was reborn with the Bunion Derby in 1928 (199 starters) and 1929 (89 starters). It was the very first footrace across

RUNNING TO EXTREMES

America. The races offered significant prize money. Johnny Salo, a shipyard worker from Passaic, New Jersey, distinguished himself in both races with a second- and first-place finish, respectively, in the two events. My father had plans of running across America, but this dream ended when he developed asthma in 1975. Two hundred fifty-two people have journeyed by foot across the United States over the years, starting with Edward Weston in 1909 at age 70. At age 13, I saw Don Shepard in New York finish his solo run across the country without a support crew or vehicle. He set a record of 73 days that lasted 16 years until Jacksonville, Florida, schoolteacher and coach, Jay Birmingham, completed the trek in 71 days. Jay's solo record still stands today.

One of the first annual ultrarunning races in the United States was the Providence to Boston 44- mile race held in March. The great Clarence DeMar used this race as a tune-up for the Boston Marathon. In 1928, DeMar would win both of these races. DeMar won the Boston Marathon seven times between 1911 and 1930.

The modern era of ultrarunning began in 1958 with the formation of the Road Runners Club of America (RRCA) by Browning Ross. The New York City metropolitan area and the New York Road Runners Club led the way in the revival of ultramarathon running by conducting the first series of ultrarunning races. Aldo Scandurra, a runner and leading administrator of the sport, organized these races in the early 1960s. The RRCA began the process of working with the sport's governing body, the Amateur Athletic Union (AAU), in which Aldo was the chair of the long-distance running committee. These efforts led to the first U. S. National 50-Mile Championship race in 1966 at Staten Island, New York.

Ted Corbitt was the face of the sport during those years. His duels with Jim McDonagh in the U.S. and Bernard Gomersall in England are legendary. He represented the U.S. on five occasions at the London-to-Brighton 52-mile road race. The London-to-Brighton was the de facto world championship race and dates back to 1951. South Africa's apartheid policy prevented my father from competing at the 54-mile Comrades Marathon, which dates back to 1921. Ted Corbitt also participated overseas in world record track races of 50 miles, 100 miles, and 24 hours from 1966 to 1973 when he set American records each time. The Millrose AA team of Gary Muhrcke, John Garlepp, and Norbert Sander won the London-to-Brighton team title in 1976. My father raced these gentlemen at all distances for many years. This team victory was certainly inspired by my father. The ultrarunning baton was passed from Ted Corbitt to these Millrose runners. In the 1970s, the baton was passed to Park Barner and Allan Kirik.

The first generation of women in ultrarunning occurred during the 1970s and included the following: Ruth Anderson, Natalie Cullimore, Donna Gookin, Miki Gorman, Judy Ikenberry, Sandra Kiddy, Sue Krenn, Nina Kuscsik, Marcy Schwam, Sue Ellen Trapp, and Eileen Waters. These women pioneers should never be forgotten. They passed the baton to Ann Trason and others.

This book does an excellent job of honoring Ted Corbitt and the other founding fathers of long-distance running. *Running to Extremes* will be an important part of the running history continuum for generations of participants, fans, historians, and scholars. Learn and be inspired by these great stories you're about to read. Take the baton and keep moving. The body and mind always get stronger by staying consistent and committed to a goal in running and in life.

Gary Corbitt, Curator

Ted Corbitt Archives

RUNNING TO EXTREMES

CHAPTER 1

RAY ZAHAB

When we think of Ray Zahab, a very distinct, defining image comes to mind. Close your eyes and imagine the finish line of the 2012 Badwater Ultramarathon. If you have been there, you know the magic of this final, epic climb. You have felt the tingles and the tears and experienced that greatly anticipated exhalation of breath (that you have unknowingly been holding since Lone Pine). The sheer magnitude of completing this

journey paired with the pride experienced by both runner and crew—it is a moment in time that becomes seared into our consciousness. For the two of us, the image is of Chris, standing in front of the iconic Badwater backdrop, flanked by Ray on his left side. Arm in arm they stood there, Ray with pride in his eyes, Chris with well-earned tears of joy. When the race photographer went to snap the photo, Chris beamed from ear to ear, and Ray, well, Ray just pointed his finger at Chris and smiled. It was a powerful gesture. It said, "This is not about me." It said, "This is what IT is all about." It said, "Together we can accomplish great things." This is who Ray is. He has committed his life to creating greatness in others.

Ray is one of the busiest people we know. He actually has to schedule his 10-minute "check-in" phone calls. He's kind of busy, you see, because he is changing the planet. His reach is limitless, not only through his incredible adventure racing, but also in his example as both father and husband. He inspires people to become better versions of themselves. Have you ever heard the C.S Lewis quote that goes something like, "Ray does the right thing, even when no one is watching." Well, maybe not exactly just like that, but you get the picture. With Ray it really is that simple. Ray walks the walk. He has had his share of challenges, just like we all do. We truly believe that it is through his humanity and in his humility that people are drawn to him. What we know for sure is that he is an integral part of our lives, and for that we are forever changed. Not only are we changed, we are blessed and committed to furthering his mission: To educate, to inspire, and to empower...and that fire starts anew each day that we are lucky enough to awaken, rise, and be the change.

–Erin and Chris Roman

RUNNING TO EXTREMES

MUTUAL INSPIRATION SOCIETY

By Scott Ludwig

I know a few people who gave up cigarettes when they started running. I know a couple of people who run yet still smoke cigarettes. I even know one runner who smokes cigars.

But it wasn't until I met Ray Zahab that I knew a person who stopped smoking a pack a day and went on to become one of the most recognizable ultrarunners in the world.

Ray Zahab was heading down the path toward a sedentary lifestyle when he decided at the age of 27 to change his lifestyle and become more like his brother—to do the things his brother, who was always quite the athlete—did to keep fit. Ice climbing. Rock climbing. Adventure racing. Mountain biking. Ray was trying it all, but nothing would ever stick. But that didn't stop Ray from deciding that the year he turned the big three-oh would be, as he refers to it, his year. The exact date for the launch of Ray Zahab 2.0 was January 1, 2000.

Ray quickly embraced the outdoor lifestyle, discovering he had the same engine as his brother—an engine that allowed him to do really long things. Always the kid picked last in gym class, Ray had no concept of his athletic potential. He couldn't throw a ball or ice skate, the latter keeping him from participating in the most popular sport in his native Canada, hockey. (Ray still can't skate.)

Everything changed in 2003 after Ray read an article about ultrarunning. Running was one of the few sports he didn't try. Although he could bicycle 100 miles at the drop of a hat, Ray was intimidated by anything much farther than 5 kilometers. He couldn't believe people could run distances of 31 miles...50 miles...ONE HUNDRED MILES! Once he realized many ultrarunners were simply ordinary, average people wanting to try something completely different by challenging themselves to test their limits, Ray decided to give it a try.

Ray redefined the word *try* as he literally became one of the most prominent adventure runners in the world. His exploits have taken him to the most extreme environments on the planet, including the Amazon rainforest, the Sahara Desert, and the South Pole.

The short version: Ray found his true calling in life. Now prepare yourself for the long version.

After all, Ray's been doing some really long things for the last decade, including his epic 1,200-kilometer (744 miles) run along the length of the driest desert on earth, the Atacama Desert in northern Chile in 2011. Ray's run, done completely on foot with limited daily resupplies and his camping and survival gear on his back, was completed in 20 days.

Ray's Atacama adventure will be told here, interspersed with a variety of additional information that will paint a clearer picture of the man who made the very most of life's wake-up call.

Dodging Land Mines (Day 1)

Ray began his Atacama run on the border of Peru and Chile. Forced to stay on the road for the first 5 kilometers to avoid stepping on a land mine, he managed to complete 78.5 kilometers (almost 49 miles) on the first day of his run, starting his run on the right foot.

RUNNING TO EXTREMES

Ray decided to stop dodging the land mines of everyday life 11 years earlier when he realized that feeling sorry for himself was the most unproductive thing he could do. Understanding there were a billion people in the world having it worse than him, he decided he wanted to celebrate life. Ray wasn't looking to become a great athlete, necessarily; he just wanted to do something in his life he could feel really good about. Participating in outdoor activities seemed to be just what Ray needed, as he began feeling healthier and happier about himself.

Fast forward to February of 2004. Ray decided to test his limits like those other average people doing ultras were doing. He entered the Yukon Arctic Ultra, a brisk little 100-mile jaunt through the snow while pulling a sled. Not only did he complete the entire 100 miles, *but he won the race!*

Ray's immediate and newfound success triggered his philosophy that people underestimate themselves physically, mentally, and emotionally as human beings. "It was very clear to me that day," he says. He adds that had his life not followed the path it did, he would have never experienced "that amazing day in the snow in February in the Yukon."

However, by no means was the 100 miles in the Yukon a walk in the park. In fact, Ray was actually "ready to throw in the towel" about halfway through the race when he remembered his commitment to do the best he could, so he decided to walk until he couldn't walk anymore. The plan was working up until the point he saw the finish line, at which time he decided to run. It dawned on him at that moment that he was a runner, and that's what runners do — they run.

The Heat Is On (Days 2 Through 5)

Ray covered 244.2 kilometers (151 miles) over the next four days. He was getting very little sleep at night, forced to take a detour that added 35 kilometers to his journey, battling huge headwinds, and running on two legs scorched by the heat reflecting off of the road. This was quickly becoming one of his toughest expeditions mentally. Military operations in the desert trumped Ray's original route; thus the additional distance run on a trail following the power lines. To combat the desert sun, he wore long sleeves to protect his arms and hands. Ray couldn't help but notice the scenery being eerily similar to that in the Sahara. He recommends the always-changing terrain (desert, then forest) as a "must see place."

In the fall of 2006, Ray, along with Charlie Engle and Kevin Lin, crossed the Sahara Desert on foot. Seven thousand five hundred kilometers (4,650 miles) in 111 days from the coast of Senegal Africa to their "finish line" in the Red Sea.

The three of them would pile up some incredible statistics during their epic run through the desert: 70 kilometers a day (just over 43 miles), ZERO days off, six countries, and (get upwind for this one) only TWO SHOWERS!

National Geographic tracked their expedition on the web, and Matt Damon produced the film *Running the Sahara* in an effort to raise awareness for the drinking water crisis in North Africa. After witnessing this crisis firsthand, Ray decided he would utilize his future endeavors and adventures to raise awareness and funding for causes he believed in.

RUNNING TO EXTREMES

On another note, the run emphasized what Ray had thought several years prior:

- We totally underestimate what we're capable of.
- We have no limits to what we're capable of.

After his desert odyssey, Ray and his wife, Kathy, wanted to replicate the Sahara experience for others, so they created the i2P Foundation, a clever abbreviation for "impossible to possible." The goals were short, to the point, and ever so powerful:

- Educate
- Inspire
- Empower

Ray and Kathy wanted to show 15-, 16-, and 17-year-olds what had taken Ray almost 40 years to learn: Don't underestimate yourself; you can do amazing things when you're younger; and the world is an incredible place, and you should want to learn more about it.

Ray and Kathy were definitely on to something big, and it was about to get even bigger.

Stoked (Day 6)

Ray covered 69 kilometers (about 43 miles) as he ran through an active salt lake as well as along an abandoned railroad while taking a timeout to ⋯ ⋯is support crew. As luck would have it, the support crew's ⋯ ⋯emblance to a car used in a robbery, and the police wanted ⋯ ⋯both the car and its suspicious-looking occupants. While ⋯ ⋯ring, Ray ran out of fluids, so he used the idle time to videoconference with schools that were following the live feed of the expedition. The communication with the students left Ray feeling reinvigorated, or, as he put it, "stoked."

Ray, Kathy, and Ray's best friend, Bob Cox, launched the i2P Foundation in 2008 as an organization directed towards inspiring and educating young adults between the ages of 17 and 21 through "adventure learning," a softer way of telling parents their loved ones were about to participate in a real-live expedition.

Youth ambassadors are selected from all over the world to participate in every aspect of the expedition. They plan the logistics and run and traverse the course while creating educational content and team support. Here's the punch line: All of this at *no cost* to the youth ambassador!

All of the i2P Youth Expeditions include challenge-based initiatives through an elaborate Experiential Learning program, involving thousands of students from classrooms all over the world. These students participate as active team members during the expeditions and learn through the adventure about specific subjects. This entire program—and all of the technology utilized to support it—is provided at no cost to the schools participating, as well.

If you're wondering how i2P manages to conduct these expeditions (Baffin Island, Tunisia, the Amazon, Bolivia, India, Botswana/Africa, and phenomenal Utah) at no cost, wonder no more. You've been reading how for the last several pages. To challenge himself and do things that are really extreme, Ray does one "ridiculous" expedition a year. Like being the first person to run the length of the Atacama Desert. Or running to the South Pole without any support. Or crossing Siberia, also unsupported, in the winter. Any and all endorsement deal revenue generated from these expeditions is donated to i2P. On a personal

RUNNING TO EXTREMES

level, Ray earns his living through speaking engagements. (Ray is an exceptional and exceptionally motivating speaker, by the way). A most appropriate vocation for a man whose office is Planet Earth.

The Going Gets Tough (Days 7 Through 14)

The low point of the run occurred on day 7: A severely bad blister on the instep of his left foot limited Ray to less than 8 kilometers (less than 5 miles). His team asked him to sit for the day to avoid the possibility of a severe infection. Capitalizing on his own advice to "pack something in your bag to look forward to," Ray took out his razor and shaved.

Nursing his foot for the next three days—but still managing to cover 164 kilometers (about 102 miles)—Ray encountered a meteor impact site and was chased by a pack of dogs while running through a small community.

The following four days resulted in another 233 kilometers (144 miles) and running with a Chilean running legend from Santiago, a long train passing by on a live rail system (Ray's daughter, Mia, loves trains), and temperatures in the low 120s...with heavy winds tossed in for good measure. On day 14, Ray did a lot of walking, making for a "bad day." Ever the optimist, he mentioned that bad days made the good days even better.

If there's one thing an ultrarunner knows from experience, it's that somewhere along the way you're going to hit a bad spell—that low point when quitting would be an oh-so-welcome relief from the torture you're willingly subjecting yourself to. Never was that more evident when Ray broke the speed record for trekking 1,200 kilometers (744 miles) from Hercules Inlet to the South Pole. Not only did Ray break the record by five days, he also became the first person to make the journey solely on foot (others had done it on skis, as Kevin Vallely and Richard Weber did as well while accompanying Ray on this adventure).

But *how* Ray did it is quite the tale. You had better believe he had his share of low points considering:

The training alone for this expedition—multi-hour trail runs, running while dragging a tire and wearing 30-pound packs, and training on cold and icy roads as well as snowy trails—is enough to make the average ultrarunner think twice about such a run. Ray had to secure sheet metal screws on the bottoms of both shoes so that he would have the necessary traction to traverse the snow and ice inherent in the area. Inside his shoes were linings made of blanket scraps to help keep his feet from becoming frostbitten. Ray's pack contained all of the gear essential for his survival: a titanium pot, a lightweight jacket, a first aid kit (primarily for blister treatment), a headlamp, water in flexible flasks, and electronic gear to communicate with the schools. And let's not forget Ray's only means of shelter at night: a tent!

Ray dragged a dog sled weighed down with 170 pounds of gear, all of it necessary for his protection, safety, and survival. After all, he would be facing temperatures reaching 40 degrees Fahrenheit below zero, strong headwinds, hidden crevasses that could give beneath Ray's weight in a heartbeat (on the first day Ray's sled fell through one of them, causing him to think, "what have I gotten myself into?"), and a route that was *uphill the entire way*. The route, which began at sea level, would ultimately reach 10,000 feet above sea level once the final destination—the South Pole—was reached.

Let's take a short timeout to hear some wisdom from the architect of the South Pole expedition himself:

RUNNING TO EXTREMES

We can do anything we set our minds to.

Now one more:

We need a reason besides just getting there.

Ray enjoyed using the electronic gear on his sled to communicate with the students who were eagerly following his progress. He was inspired by many of the elementary school children who were dragging their sleds across the schoolyard, pretending they were Ray, Richard, or Kevin (the latter two being Ray's companions on the trek). It was pretty apparent that Ray and friends were inspiring the children as well.

Ray enjoyed answering the questions from the students.

Q: Where do you sleep?

A: On tents secured low to the ground so the strong winds won't blow them away. (They also slept on their sleds during the day, taking short catnaps in frigid 40-below temperatures.)

Q: What do you eat?

A: Butter and bacon—since they have about a million calories (said in jest, the point being the food they ingested needed to be loaded with calories), and we're each burning 8,500 calories a day.

Q: Do you carry batteries with you?

A: No; the equipment is powered by rechargeable batteries.

Q: Do the three of you get along?

A: Yes, and that's a good thing since we will occasionally be sticking a big needle in one another to drain infected blisters.

You can see how the students were keeping Ray's spirits alive! Knowing they were listening to their exploits at home just added more fuel to Ray's ever-burning fire.

Ray took two things from his South Pole expedition:

- We can make the impossible possible.
- I'm learning this (we can make the impossible possible) at 40.

Imagine being 13 years old, hearing those words and *believing them*.

Second Wind (Day 15)

Today's distance (60 kilometers, or 37 miles) wasn't nearly as relevant as Ray's perspective. Ray woke up with a new resolve and a positive outlook. What brought about his dramatic but necessary mood swing at this late stage of the expedition? A simple telephone call home to speak with his wife and daughter. His most potent tool for today's run? Hearing his wife and daughter say they're proud of him.

Following today's run, Ray simply said, "today was one of the best."

Looking over some of Ray's other accomplishments, it appears he has made more than one reinvigorating phone call home in his life, perhaps when Ray ran an average of 80 kilometers (50 miles) a day for 13 days in the 13 Canadian provinces and territories or when he ran the three coastal

RUNNING TO EXTREMES

trails of Canada (400 kilometers, or 248 miles) back to back over the course of eight days. There was also an over 2,000-kilometer run across the Gobi Desert, a 1,000-kilometer run across the Patagonian Desert, a choice of four different crossings of the Baffin Island in the Canadian Arctic, as well as multiple youth expeditions all over the world.

Ray's desire in life—to make a very positive change on this planet—is personified in his presentations that are constantly in demand. After all, what organization couldn't use a pick-me-up or a shot-in-the-arm from the Ray Zahab Collection? Here are a few who have:

- International Olympic Committee World Conference
- Economist World
- World Affairs Council
- TED
- Idea City

Ray is a draw on television as well, including appearances on CNN, *The Hour*, CBC, CTV, BBC, *The Tonight Show With Jay Leno,* and *Discovery*.

Aside from i2P, Ray donates portions of his time to other organizations he believes in. Among his many credentials, Ray was a member of the board of directors of the Ryan's Well Foundation, an athletic ambassador and board member of ONEXONE.org, and a representative of Spread the Net.

For his contributions all over the world, Ray was the recipient of the OneXOne Difference Award in 2007 and the Torchbearers Award in 2010. He is also a fellow of the Royal Geographical Society and Canadian Geographical Society. In 2012, Ray was invited by the Minister of Environment in Mongolia to join their Internal Advisory Committee.

Ray has also carved out enough time in his busy life to write two successful books chronicling his life and adventures: *Running for My Life* and (for younger readers) *Running to Extremes*.

For Ray Zahab, every day has the potential to be one of the best.

Cruise Control (Days 16 Through 19)

Covering 248 kilometers (154 miles) in four days in an admitted "hypnotic trance" gives the illusion that this stretch may have been the simplest, the most automatic of the entire journey.

Since the support crew's car was experiencing more problems with its battery than Ray was having running through a blistering hot desert, perhaps the simplicity wasn't merely an illusion, but rather a reality.

Ray insists the success or failure of accomplishing your goals is determined by mental preparation, which is "90% mental and 10% in your head."

If anyone knows that to be true, it's Ray.

The mental fortitude required for running the length of frozen Lake Baikal in Siberia—650 kilometers (403 miles)—in 13 days in the dead of winter without any support whatsoever is almost beyond comprehension for the average marathoner, let alone the occasional jogger.

The psychological warfare going on inside the head when running the 237 kilometers (147 miles) from the north park boundary to the south park boundary of Death Valley National Park—totally off-road and with temperatures creeping above 120 degrees—is practically unimaginable.

RUNNING TO EXTREMES

The emotional battles being waged within yourself when running 1,200 kilometers (744 miles) in 20 days across the driest desert on earth with minimal daily resupply and camping gear on your back is almost impossible to fathom.

But Ray has run on frozen Lake Baikal and through insanely hot Death Valley. And in one more day he will complete his trek across the Atacama Desert.

Challenge yourself. Test your limits.

Happy Birthday, Ray! (Day 20)

Nineteen long, exhausting days. Enormous, painful blisters. Ankle-deep sand. Additional mileage caused by unexpected obstacles. Blistering hot pavement.

Then, on the 20th and final day, another 87 kilometers (54 miles).

Not the greatest way to celebrate your birthday.

That is to say, unless your name is Ray Zahab; in which case it's EXACTLY the way to celebrate your birthday.

As I listened to Ray's webcast of his Atacama Desert journey, I noticed his voice maintained the same level of excitement and enthusiasm each and every day during his 20-day adventure.

As Ray reached the end of his run, he pointed out that the main purpose of his expeditions is to benefit the youth of today. He then held up a tiny stuffed monkey he carried in his pack for the entire 1,200 kilometers, complements of the clandestine efforts of his daughter, Mia.

By the expression on his face as he held the monkey up to the camera, Ray appeared as impressed by his daughter's expression of love and support as he did with what he accomplished over the past 20 days.

Ray Zahab is fostering a new level as well as a new *generation* of interest into the world of expedition and adventure running and the amazing planet we live on. Ray's intent has always been to make "a very positive change on this planet," and from the looks of things, he's well on his way toward achieving his goal.

Ray Zahab's résumé might look something like this:

- Adventure runner
- Expedition leader
- Volunteer
- Husband
- Father
- i2P Founder
- Speaker
- Dreamer
- Inspiration to children and young adults around the globe

As passionate as Ray is about today's youth, that last one could easily have read:

- *Inspired by* children and young adults around the globe

After all, in Ray Zahab's neighborhood, inspiration is a two-way street.

RUNNING TO **EXTREMES**

CHAPTER 2

MIKE SMITH

MIKE SMITH

I've known the "Younger" Mike for many years, and we have the special bond of having shared quite a few running miles. We have had great uplifting moments and also some low, depressing, and painful moments. That is the bond that many marathon and ultra miles on roads and trails produce.

Mike is a great optimist. He is stubborn, analytical, and a great planner—all characteristics of a great ultrarunner. For example, before a run, I would get in the mail a laminated card with time, running pace, aid stations, and projected finishing time. All of this well before the event.

Something that our running buddies and I have learned is not to let Mike loose in a grocery store before an ultra (especially if he has your credit card). He can buy half the store even though in the event itself he will use a tenth of the supplies.

Mike wants to run all of the 100-milers in the USA, and if somebody can, he should be the one doing it. The ultrarunning boom is producing more and more 100-milers all the time, so Mike should stay busy for the time being. Mike has proven that running three 100-milers a week apart is possible. If anyone can run all of those 100-milers, my money's on Mike.

I feel privileged to have shared the trail with him. He has become the ultrarunner that we all want to be: able to tackle any distance, on any terrain, regardless of the weather conditions—finish.

Mike is indeed an ultrarunner.

–Andy Velazco

RUNNING TO **EXTREMES**

IRON MIKE

By Craig Snapp

Mike Smith is a marathon and ultra man. Yet since there is no money in the sport (unless one is an uber-elite athlete), he is definitely not a pro. However, he is *pro*lific. He is *pro*ficient. He is *pro*digious. He is *pro*active. (Okay, well, maybe that last word doesn't really fit, but it does have a nice sound to it.) Captain Obvious states that running is not about compiling numbers, and, as always, he is correct. However, numbers can be an interesting by-product to some. And since I'm one of those "some," please allow me to introduce my favorites of Mike's Mathematical Amalgamation:

In the last 19 years, he's completed 377 marathons or ultras. (He's also completed six others that he doesn't include because they were not "official" races!)

- 93 of those races were 100-miles or more.
- He's finished a marathon or ultra on a Saturday, then another on Sunday, 11 times.
- He's completed 100-mile races on three consecutive weekends.
- He's done a marathon or ultra in all 50 states and is within five of the second lap around.
- He's run a marathon or ultra on all seven continents.
- He's done the Umstead 100-Mile Endurance Run 15 times, and counting.
- And to mix things up a bit, he's completed three Ironman races.

Personally fascinated with the mind's contribution to all of these numbing numbers, I asked Mike how much of his success was due to his "gray wrinkled matter." He answered, "I'm sure you are thinking mental versus physical prowess when asking that question. I tell folks all the time I have never been a very talented or well-trained athlete. As you can see [Mike had shared with me a list of all of his marathon or ultra races], I race much more than I have time to train and am usually a mid-to-back-of-the-pack finisher. However, I think I have a determination level that gets me through some events when other more talented and better-trained competitors just decide they don't want to go on any farther. I have literally been right there with some of those folks when they talked themselves into that decision. I'm not immune either, but can probably count on one hand the number of times I have just mentally thrown in the towel."

Looking at the aforementioned list of his finishes, I realized they were all marathons or ultras beginning in 1995, making me curious about what had preceded that. "My father was advocating running for fitness in the 1960s. I can remember him taking us to the local track and running 'long' distances—at that time anything more than a mile—when we were still in grade school. My first running award was a small plaque from a local YMCA for running a cumulative distance of 100 miles. [Note: This may be when Mike got the phrase "100-Miles" tattooed onto his medulla oblongata!] I'm sure it took several months. Sometime around junior high [the late 1960s], I stopped running and started swimming competitively. I really didn't return to running until the late 1980s when I was working in Baton Rouge, Louisiana. I had a friend at work that wanted to run at lunch, and we would do that during the week with longer (three or more miles) runs on the weekend on the Louisiana State University campus. I remember my first competitive run was as part of a Corporate Cup Relay team in 1991. Shortly thereafter, I relocated to Mobile, Alabama, and continued to run there. My longest distance was

RUNNING TO EXTREMES

the Azalea Trail (10K) race every year. I was working with someone who lived in Orlando, Florida, at the time and wanted to run a marathon to help with his weight-loss program. As an incentive I told him if he ever thought he was capable of doing it I would try it with him. I honestly never thought he would want to do it. Then he called and said he was ready to run the Disney Marathon in January 1995 [when Mike was 37]. Good to my word, I signed up. I had no idea how to train, but I think I may have managed to work up to a long run of 15 miles before the race. [He finished it in 4:19, a 9:50 per mile pace.] You can see from my race list, it took a year before I decided to try it again."

Still focusing on that list, I noticed his back-to-back (Saturday–Sunday) marathons or ultras (done 11 times) and his back-to-back-to-back weekends of 100-mile races. Being very intrigued with this part of his race résumé, I asked how this idea had become a "Chosen Challenge." Mike responded, "I think you have hit upon an important point. I believe I have always needed a challenge to keep me going. I'm not sure there would have been a point to accumulating those races you see on that list if they had not been in pursuit of a personal challenge at the time. Here are some examples of past and current challenge opportunities." (I'd referred to portions of a few of Mike's examples earlier.)

- Finish a marathon or longer distance in all 50 states and D.C.—Completed in November 2001 and currently only a few states away from completing challenge for a second time.
- Finish a marathon or longer distance on all seven continents—Completed in November 2015.
- Finish the Rocky Mountain Slam—Done!
- Finish 10 Umstead 100-Mile Endurance Runs for 1,000 total miles—Did 15 for 1,500 miles, and now it's kind of a streak.
- Finish an Ironman—Did three so far (yet he hates that bike!).

- The HURT 100—Will continue to be a challenge for him to try to finish each year.
- Continue streak of completing all Flying Pig Marathons—Did 17 and counting.
- Complete the Grand Slam—Completed in the summer of 2014.
- Dream Goal: Finish every established 100-mile race. ("They just keep coming up with too many new ones! I'm still dreaming!")
- Realistic Goal: Complete one hundred 100-mile races—Not counting the Levee Runs (130 miles; Mike's done it twice) or Badwater (135 miles; Mike's done it once).
- Determine how many 100-mile races can be completed on consecutive weekends - Completed up to three at this point in time. (Mike does not recommend this!)
- Finish at least 15 100-mile races in a year—Completed 16 in 2014!

"As you can see," Mike said, "I don't think I'll ever run out of challenge opportunities!"

Focusing on the 100-mile races, I noted that he'd done 93 races that distance (or longer) and asked if he knew where that might place him on a list of folks who'd done this inspiring uber-idiocy. "Good question that I don't know the answer to. I am aware of several folks who have done 100 or more 100s. Stan Jensen, creator of the Run100s.com website might know."

At the beginning of Mike's racing career, there was a very high percentage of races that were marathons, and recently there has been an increasing percentage that were 100-mile races. So I asked how he decided to transition from mostly marathons to mostly 100s, and if there was a known antidote. He said, "Part of it was looking for that additional challenge opportunity. I'm always looking enviously at that next greater distance event or tougher race. I really had no idea what I was doing when I signed up for that first 50-mile race, but it ended up being my fastest time at that distance ever. If I had known what I was doing, I probably would have run slower!" (He completed 50 miles in 9:04, which is a 10:52 per mile pace.)

He's raced Badwater once (and been a crew member several times) and finished in 45:12. Therefore, I asked how long 45:12 *seems* to take? (And please answer to the nearest month!) Mike answered, "Time actually went by too fast. My crew would tell you I drove them all nuts, constantly doing the race math and calculating pace, distance, and predicted finishing time. The miles just take forever in the hottest sections. Again, my year was an experiment, and I think we got much better as a team in later years. Team dynamics and preparation are critical to your success in that environment. It's always a relief just to have the race start and, as a crew member, to focus on finishing or supporting the runner."

Thinking about his crewing experience, I asked what that was like, and if there were any aspects that are actually tougher than being the runner. He responded, "Crewing can be difficult, but I always really tried to have fun with it, too. You just feel a lot of responsibility for the runner and don't want to be the one to screw up their race. But, I would go back in a heartbeat!"

Mike's done Western States a couple times, and that reminded me of a story told by fellow Darkside Running Club member, Al Barker. He was pulled out of that race at the 28-mile checkpoint for missing the cutoff time and said it was a "mercy killing!" Sharing that, I then asked Mike if he could understand or identify with Al's description. He said, "Definitely! I wasn't pulled from the race, but I dropped at mile 85 in Hardrock one year to walk out with my pacer, who was a bit hypothermic and having back spasms. While it was disappointing to stop after 85 miles, I was getting close to the cutoff, and it didn't take much convincing for me to decide to bail! Like that mental thing we were talking about earlier. I had a similar experience with a good friend at the ill-fated Reactor 100 in Georgia. We stopped at 53 miles after battling through some rain and mud that just made it miserable. I probably could have finished, but my friend's decision was all the encouragement I needed."

He's done the Great Levee Run (130 miles) a couple of times, so I asked what were the best parts and the worst parts. Mike responded, "By far the best is the group of folks we invite to do it. Crewing (usually the wives) and some home-cooked Cajun-influenced food selections also contribute to the great atmosphere. The worst are probably some large gravel rock sections on the levee and what can be hot temperatures in New Orleans on the second morning of the race for those last remaining miles."

No matter how super any man's list of accomplishments might be, there have to be some races that come closer than others to planting the Kryptonite Kiss. With that in mind, Mike was asked if he had any favorite examples of his mind saying, "There-Ain't-No-Way-I'm-Gonna-Finish-This-Mother," then later his mind asking, "Was-That-Really-The-Freakin'-Finish-Line-I-Just-Stumbled-Across!?" He answered, "Hands down, my last two finishes at HURT. Both were exactly 11 minutes under the cutoff. It took me six years just to get my first 100-mile finish there. Hardrock is tough, but the fact that they give you 48 hours to get it done means HURT has been more of a challenge for me. Some folks won't believe that, knowing how difficult Hardrock or even Badwater can be."

Stories of runners who have seen things that aren't actually of this world are legendary. One source claims that during the Desert Run of Moses, he saw stuff that no one else had ever seen, partly because of extreme fatigue and inadequate electrolyte replenishment. Mike was asked when it came to the Hallucination Monster if he had any knowledge of said beast. He said, "I am sure it has happened in a few races, but Badwater stands out. My pacer at the time will tell you I thought I was running through a neighborhood on a road through a desert in the middle of the night. I saw houses, fences, bushes, and trees. I just couldn't understand why people would live in the middle of a desert. It's also not unusual for me to think I see various animals or people along a trail at night. It usually turns out to be a rock, bush, or stick that has morphed into some living shape until I get closer."

With all that he has accomplished, I was curious if he had any short- or long-term goals that he might care to share beyond what he'd already listed. He responded, "I really want to keep running, with my friends, preferably, until we have to give it up and crew for everyone else. Ultrarunning is much more of a 'communal' experience than marathoning. I did have friends who I would meet for marathons, but I have literally run every step of a 100-mile race with some of my best friends, and you really get to know each other and experience a lot of ups and downs when you do that with someone. It's also great just coming across someone on a trail after running for miles with no one and being able to share a few moments with them. The aid station folks, pacers, and crew members critical to our success are usually a great bunch with which to interact. But, I digress. I have a group of friends who get excited about challenges like running across the Grand Canyon, finding trails in national parks (Rocky Mountain National Park last summer), circumventing the base of Mount Rainier, and other similar adventure runs that have nothing to do with a formal event. I plan to try to work those into my goals for the future."

Given that some of his performances are out of this world, he was asked if the Internet rumor was true—that he was going to be the race director for the first running event on the lunar surface, which will be called the 262-Mile Memorial Michael Jackson MOON-WALK/Run. Mike said, "You won't catch me directing anything other than an informal get-together. My hat is off to those race directors who make it possible for guys like me to have fun on a weekend. I *am* up for a race in a remote location, and zero gravity might be just what my joints need right now!"

As a wise man once said, "The more things change, the more things... change!" He was right, brothers and sisters! The loneliness of the long-distance runner has changed: The London Marathon accepts 45,000 runners but receives applications from over 200,000! The 100-mile race scene has changed to where it's no longer a rare outpost!

Yet there are indeed some things that stay the same. I believe that one of those will be the statement: Mike Smith is a marathon–ultra man!

RUNNING TO **EXTREMES**

CHAPTER 3

AMY PALMIERO-WINTERS

For several months I have been asked to try and write down a couple of words about Amy: who she is, what kind of person she is, and what she means to me. Easier said than done.

I have been really contemplating how to do her justice. How do you even begin to describe a phenomenon like Amy? Athlete, superstar, supermom, and, let me add, incredible friend.

Amy is one of the most important people in my life. She has become one of my best friends and works with me in making a difference in other peoples' lives.

Amy and I have tackled some of the most difficult prosthetic challenges known to the prosthetic industry that clearly indicate we are a team. Amy is also the most accomplished amputee athlete in the world, male or female.

For over six years, we have worked together in a clinical setting helping others who suffer from the loss of a limb to live life without limitation. For over eight years, we have been an unstoppable team, defying the odds and rewriting prosthetic history.

As a caregiver and in a clinical setting, Amy works and runs my company as the director of A Step Ahead Prosthetics, acting as a team leader to motivate people with limb loss and develop new ways to open doors and allow them the same opportunities she was given (it's always so personal!).

If you think you can imagine what an ultrarunner, triathlete and world competitor would be like to work with, let me just say, you can't possibly imagine. She never quits or takes no for an answer, and she always puts the best interests of the patients first. As for me, I have been a world

RUNNING TO EXTREMES

leader in what I do for 28 years, but every day, when working or racing alongside Amy, she has taught me how to push myself to a place where I never thought prosthetics would go.

She believes in me and shares my desire to help others overcome challenges, all the while competing against the best athletes in the world on a regular basis.

Because of all of this—because she's just Amy and that's the way she is—I consider myself to be her biggest fan.

–Erik Schaffer

SECOND CHANCES

By Scott Ludwig

> *My gift is in running.*
>
> –Amy Palmiero-Winters, Runner

Amy Palmiero-Winters started running as a child. In fact, she ran her first race when she was eight years old. She enjoyed many other sports as well: swimming, skiing, baseball, and softball, to name a few. But she always thought running was her true gift. In the late 1980s, Amy ran competitively in high school in her hometown of Meadville, Pennsylvania, setting the stage for a bright and promising future in the world of running. Amy enjoyed being part of a team—a team committed to giving everything toward a common goal. Her dad, an exceptional athlete himself, taught Amy to finish what she started.

It would be almost two decades later before Amy would realize the potential of her gift and how she could use her gift to inspire the lives of others. One other thing worth mentioning: Amy had no idea of the role that fate would play toward the realization of her gift. She did know, however, that she had to finish what she started, and, fate notwithstanding; she intended to do just that.

In 1992, when Amy was 19 years old, a friend bet her she couldn't run a marathon. Although she didn't know what a marathon was at the time, hadn't done any training, and the longest run of her life was only four miles, she took the bet. Her debut marathon time of 3:24 not only won the bet, but it also qualified her for the prestigious Boston Marathon as well.

RUNNING TO EXTREMES

The next year, Amy ran a solid 3:16 at Boston, an impressive time for most runners but even more so for a capricious 20-year-old. Little did she know at the time that it would remain her personal best marathon time for the next 13 years, because one year later fate put its finger on the pause button of Amy's future.

> *You'll never run again.*
>
> –Various doctors to Amy in 1994

In 1994, Amy was enjoying one of her few non-cardio forms of recreation, riding her Harley Davidson 883, when a car struck her from the side, resulting in a horrific accident that crushed Amy's left foot. Although doctors initially wanted to amputate, Amy insisted on giving her foot a chance. After two months in the hospital, doctors came to the realization that Amy's running career was over.

Despite a foot that was curling, atrophying, three sizes smaller than it was prior to the accident, and no longer fitting into a normal shoe, she ran the Columbus Marathon one year later in 4:03. "Out of spite," Amy says. As it turned out, it was also the swan song for Amy's damaged leg.

Over the next three years, Amy had 27 surgeries performed to correct the damage. However, in 1997, the decision was made to amputate Amy's leg three inches below the knee. One of her doctors apologized for not amputating her foot the day of the accident. Amy would not run again for three years.

> *Compared with the problems some people have, this is like a hangnail.*
>
> –Amy Palmiero-Winters, Determined Athlete

Amy's close friends were concerned about her emotional state of mind as the date for the amputation drew near. Her family knew better; they knew Amy was one tough nut to crack. Although being born three months premature and weighing a mere 2 pounds 11 ounces, the doctors allowed Amy's parents to take her home from the hospital when she weighed just over 4 pounds. Maybe it was because the doctors didn't appreciate Amy constantly kicking the inside of the incubator, but more likely it was because they never had to deal with a newborn showing that much strength and determination before.

After the amputation, Amy tried multiple prosthetic legs with very little success. Her insurance company denied Amy's first prosthesis because it was deemed "not medically necessary," so she had to pay for it personally before she could pick it up. Amy did not receive any physical therapy, counseling, or gait training. Adding insult to injury, the prosthetic leg was a terrible fit; apparently her leg had been amputated "too long," and Amy was unable to fit running components underneath it. In time, she incurred a bone infection, resulting in the loss of more of her leg; the doctors insisted a new socket was not necessary, so Amy continued to experiment with different options.

In 2004, she finally got a prosthetic leg she could run on, although it was only made for walking and caused large blisters where the prosthesis attached to her leg. Despite the limitation, Amy managed to run a 1:57 at the National Leg Amputee Half Marathon Championship in 2005.

RUNNING TO EXTREMES

That same year, while five months pregnant, Amy competed in her first triathlon. Soon afterward, she finished third in the Paratriathlon National Championships—with a walking prosthesis, duct tape, socket padding and a rotary tool. Not long after that, Amy won her class in the Paratriathlon World Championships.

But that wasn't enough for Amy.

In 2006, after searching for the right prosthetist for nine years, she made an appointment with A Step Ahead. Amy's life was one radical change after another and was about to change once more. This time, perhaps, it was the most radical change of all.

Without a doubt, she is mentally the toughest person I've ever seen.

–Erik Schaffer, President of A Step Ahead

When Erik Schaffer asked Amy what her goals were, it was the first time in her life she had been asked the question by a prosthetist. When Amy replied she wanted to run 100 miles, he didn't blink an eye.

It wasn't long before Amy ran her first marathon as an amputee in 3:26, breaking the record for a female below-the-knee amputee by 26 minutes. Soon Amy moved her family closer to the A Step Ahead facility in Hicksville, New York. The move paid off in the way of upgraded equipment and a specific training regimen that led to a 3:04 Chicago Marathon, the best-known time for an amputee—of either gender. A world record in an Olympic distance triathlon in New York City and her second triathlon World Championship (Switzerland) rounded out a year in which she proved she could do anything she ever did on two legs on only one—and faster.

Readers of *Runner's World* magazine were so inspired by learning about Amy's accomplishments that she was selected as the magazine's first-ever Reader's Choice Hero in 2007.

Prior to A Step Ahead, Amy's mindset was seeing herself as more of an individual rather than being part of a team. Schaffer's confidence in Amy changed that, and she realized it was easier to believe in her abilities when someone else believed in them as well.

> *Everybody has something they love in life. I love running.*
>
> –Amy Palmiero-Winters, Extraordinary Athlete

Actions speak louder than words. Running with a prosthetic leg that she puts on every day ("like putting on a pair of eyeglasses," she says), Amy has competed in races ranging in distance from 31 miles to 135 miles as well as triathlons from the Olympic distance to the Ironman distance, setting many world records (in her running class) along the way.

In 2009, Amy was the first female at the Heartland Spirit of the Prairie 100-Mile Race (18:54:13) and earned the USATF Athlete of the Week honors. With her performance, she also became the first female amputee to qualify for the Western States Endurance Run, which she ran the following year and finished in 27:43:10. Before that, there was Amy's performance at a 24-hour race in Arizona on New Year's Eve 2009, an event she won outright by running 130.04 miles while beating the second-place finisher by almost 14 miles. It was the first time in history an amputee had won an ultramarathon. But it wasn't quite as simple as that.

RUNNING TO EXTREMES

Amy had pushed a small child in a wheelchair in a marathon in December. When she began running in the 24-hour event a few weeks later, she began to notice a pain in her lower back she couldn't understand. Four hours into the 24-hour race, she realized her urine was dark red. A friend encouraged her to keep running. "You'll be fine," she said. But Amy wasn't fine. Her prosthetic leg had "echoed" itself out, as the carbon fiber could only take so much pounding; once so many miles were put on it, it was simply no longer able to absorb the shock. So the shock from Amy hitting the ground went straight up through her body into her lower back and jarred her internal organs. Doctors later told her she was bleeding internally for almost 23 hours.

In spite of it all, she literally pounded out 130 miles and said, "It was a fun and emotional race because you focus on trying to be such a great example for your children. [Son, Carson, and daughter, Madilynn, were in Arizona to watch their mommy run.] At the 22-hour mark, you're just wasted, and you don't really have much left to do. It was exciting and basically one of my better races in spite of everything. So it was so exciting just for the fact my kids could say I was a cool mom and also able to represent my country."

As for Amy representing her country, her performance in Arizona qualified her for a spot on the U.S. National 24-Hour World Championship team (the women's U.S. national team finished in fourth place; Amy placed fourth among the U.S. women with 124 miles in a performance she didn't consider as one of her best). As Roy Pirrung, president of the American Ultrarunning Association and team leader for the World Championships, so eloquently said at the time, "It's sort of like Jackie Robinson breaking the racial barrier in professional baseball. I think it's that high of an impact." The Amateur Athletic Union apparently felt the same way, awarding Amy their coveted Sullivan Award and recognizing her as the nation's Amateur Athlete of the Year for 2009.

What to do for an encore? Amy's story of her 2010 Western States Endurance Run experience should answer that question. Her story is enough to give anyone goose bumps:

I ran Western States to complete the goal of a gentleman who was a top athlete in the 1980s who also lost his leg in a motorcycle accident. I heard his story about him being the first athlete with a prosthetic leg to run Western States; he got to mile 35 before he was forced to drop out. He said it was one of the hardest things he had ever done and said he had to go back and finish it. The same year he was training for the Ironman and was hit by a cement bucket and killed. Somebody told me his story, and I decided to finish his story for him. I qualified for Western States and ran it for him and gave the finisher's belt buckle to his widow and their daughter. Another young lady running in that race heard of the story and within a few days of me being home she sent me her *buckle. So I have to go back and get my own [buckle].*

Amy ran a triathlon in Connecticut held in the gentleman's honor a few days after she returned home from Western States. At some point in the race the competitors pass by a large photograph of him. That was where Amy gave his family her buckle.

To Amy that is what running is all about. "I know some people see me and think I am one of those crazy ultrarunners. I'm really not. It may seem like I am, but I run for many different reasons. I run to help people. I run to inspire people. Like if I'm out there running 100 miles and someone sees me along the way, they might encounter something that presents itself as a challenge, and they can think back to seeing me, and it can help them realize they can get through whatever they're facing. Running is a part of what I am and a part of my identity, but I also like to help people. Little girls with cancer think if the lady with the prosthetic leg can run 100 miles, then I can walk one. I do it for many reasons."

RUNNING TO **EXTREMES**

Amy began 2011 by winning the Long Haul 100-Mile Run (Florida) in 23:59:16 in January. Six months later she would find herself in Death Valley for her greatest challenge yet.

> *The temperature of my prosthetic leg reached 166 degrees.*
>
> –Amy Palmiero-Winters, Relentless Competitor

In the summer of 2011, Amy had the distinction of becoming the first female amputee to finish the Badwater Ultramarathon—a 135-mile footrace from Badwater, California, to the portals of Mount Whitney. The route just happens to take the competitors through the middle of Death Valley, the site of the highest temperature ever recorded in the United States some 88 years earlier: 134 degrees Fahrenheit. One year earlier, Amy got a glimpse of what the race would be like when she started the race but failed to finish, realizing she would need to have her A-game not only to finish but also to avoid serious injury along the way.

Those who knew Amy best understood that perhaps her greatest enemy might very well be herself–specifically, her ability to block out pain, something that could ultimately lead to her demise. In her first foray at Badwater in 2010, Amy developed third-degree burns on her residual limb while running almost 100 miles in the most adverse of conditions— temperatures in the neighborhood of 120 degrees Fahrenheit.

However, Amy wasn't satisfied with a "close but no cigar" performance in her first Badwater, so she was intent on going forward and getting to the finish line at the portals of Mount Whitney. To do it for the children who lost limbs and show them what's possible if you put your heart and soul into it. Beyond that, Amy wanted to do it for anyone and everyone who face obstacles each and every day. "We all face obstacles; mine is pretty obvious," Amy says. "Whether you run or not, you'll see me out there doing my best to overcome it. I hope it will give you the courage to believe in yourself and follow your dreams."

In 2011, Amy reached Badwater's finish line in a respectable time of 41 hours and 26 minutes. She returned one year later. At one point during the race, the temperature of her prosthetic leg was measured at 166 degrees Fahrenheit; dry ice had to be dropped into it to cool it down so Amy could continue. And continue she did. Amy finished in 36 hours and 49 minutes, bettering her time from the prior year by almost five full hours.

What is truly amazing is how Amy prepared for her third Badwater by doing Cross Fit—a mix of aerobic exercise, gymnastics, and weight lifting. She immediately noticed it made a difference in her running. With a long training run of only 20 miles prior to Badwater, she relied on her Cross Fit and two-per-week track workouts to carry her through Death Valley. Perhaps "fearless determination" needs to be added into that equation as well.

As Amy so eloquently states: "Everything I have accomplished has always been done together as a team. I don't think you can really do the things you want to do as far as winning awards or doing things by yourself. It's always done with a team effort; there are always people behind you. Without the spirit of those around you, it's tough for us to do what we do. Especially in [extreme] races that are so long you require a team. You need all of those people behind you."

RUNNING TO **EXTREMES**

> *The strongest mental game you will ever come across, in any athlete, anywhere.*
>
> –Erik Schaffer, president of A Step Ahead

When Amy originally faced the toughest challenge of her life immediately after her tragic accident, she had a choice between falling into a deep depression or moving on, as there was nothing that could be done to bring her leg back. It came as no surprise to those who knew Amy that her love for running would lead her to the second option: moving on.

Amy's efforts paid off, not only through her numerous athletic achievements, but also through her work with A Step Ahead, the New York prosthetics and orthotics company based in Long Island, New York. According to the company's website, their mission "is to give our patients the tools, information and resources necessary to allow them to achieve their goals" and "provide healthcare, advocacy and educational services so that our patients can live life without limitations!"

The company supported Amy the athlete with customized running prosthetics and professional coaching. As for Amy's team she referenced earlier, it included Erik Schaffer, president of A Step Ahead; exercise physiologist, Bob Otto; and sports nutritionist, Pam Nisevich.

It wasn't long before she was rewarding their confidence in her with world record performances. Aside from qualifying for the Western States Endurance Run, the U.S. National Ultrarunning Team, and winning the Sullivan Award, Amy also won ESPN's ESPY Award as the nation's outstanding female athlete with a disability in 2010.

Erik Schaffer also exhibited confidence in Amy's ability to inspire others as well, as he soon named Amy as the clinical director of both Team Step Ahead and Junior Step Ahead.

Somehow Amy still is able to find time for sharing her hopes and dreams with children who have been thrown life's curve ball: the loss of a limb due to cancer, birth defects, trauma, or various diseases. Amy's belief is that getting started in life is difficult enough, but starting without an arm or a leg only serves to make it that much tougher.

Amy's message is one she shares with all children: Be the best you can be, have courage, never give up, and never quit. The children are fortunate to have someone to look up to who not only leads by example, but also does everything in her power to help them find what makes them happy and feel good so that they have something to focus on as they experience tough times. "It helps them take the necessary steps to keep moving forward," Amy said. By getting the children involved in sports, she can concentrate on developing the self-confidence they may have otherwise lost as a result of losing a limb at an early age.

Amy soon founded the One Step Ahead Foundation to provide even more opportunities for children with physical disabilities. The foundation's mission statement is pure Amy:

The One Step Ahead Foundation is a not-for-profit organization dedicated to giving young children with physical disabilities positive experiences through sports to build confidence, courage and friendship, increase self-esteem, and create a better sense of self-worth all while giving them a positive experience they will use throughout the rest of their lives. This foundation will especially focus on children with limb loss and provide them with the means to participate in various athletics.

RUNNING TO EXTREMES

Amy adds: "I help children who have lost limbs due to cancer, birth defects, or other things. Because sports were such a big part of my growing up and kind of what gave me confidence to get over what happened to me, I work with children who have steered away from sports because of their prosthetics. I get them involved in sports because it helps them build self-confidence."

Amy insists on giving back. She speaks to lots of organizations and runs in a lot of races to spread her message of hope. She'll visit a school or a hospital and speak directly to the kids about overcoming obstacles, setting goals, doing what they enjoy, and following their dreams. Then she'll meet with a child—usually one confined to a wheelchair—and ask him or her to be her teammate for the race. She'll push them in the race and assign them the job of coming up with some athletic goals by the time the two of them reach the finish line. She does it, as she says, "to spark the child's interest and help them move on in life, be confident and not let anything stop them." In other words, to do what Amy did.

> **My children are my first priority.**
>
> –Amy Winters-Palmiero, Mother

Amy refers to her two children as "my best of everything." She says, "As far as anything you do in life you can have all these awards, world's best this-and-that and trophies, but what it comes down to is this: At the end of the day, for me the best thing is for me to be a good mom. I make sure I do the best at what I do, whether it be working with people or raising my children."

Amy raises her children on her own. As for them being budding athletes, Amy says, "I don't know yet. I guess time will tell. They are very talented and have natural abilities. Whether they will choose to pursue specific sports, I'm not sure yet. They tell me all the time they don't want their foot to look like mine, however." Through it all, Amy's optimism and good nature always seem to find a way to peer through her otherwise tough exterior. After all, it's virtually impossible to keep a spirit the size of Amy's hidden for long.

Amy does most of her training after the children go to bed for the night and the babysitter comes over. "It's what I have to do; it's no big deal," she says. When asked what kind of mileage she's running outside of racing, Amy says, "None, really. I go to work, try to get a workout after that, come home and fix dinner, make sure the homework gets done, hang out with the kids, and do some training once the sitter comes over." As for weekends: "That's when I make sure I give my kids their time to shine." On the weekends that Amy competes, her children and their aunt accompany her. The aunt watches Carson and Madilynn while Amy competes. Amy likes to do well if for no other reason than to demonstrate to her children what they're capable of accomplishing if they set their minds to it. Given Amy's track record of outstanding performances, it appears her plan has been working just fine.

> **The woman simply didn't want to sit next to me.**
>
> –Amy Palmiero-Winters, Human Being

Amy says, "I tell the kids that if there is that one thing that makes you feel good inside, and no matter what happens during your day or what happens at school, at home, or with your friends, go do that one thing, and let it make you feel good. If you have a bad day, and you love art, go draw a picture."

Amy experienced a little bit of both—good as well as bad—after a race in 2009. Her story:

I ran the Heartland 100 in 2009; that was my first 100-mile race, and I won it. I crossed the finish line early in the morning, and no one other than the volunteer recording my time was there to see me. I received a large trophy attached to a big rock. After a quick shower at the hotel, I took my trophy and hopped on the plane to fly home. When I boarded the plane, I asked if I could put my trophy on the floor and my backpack in the overhead compartment. I was wearing a running skirt, so my prosthetic was very much out in the open. A woman who obviously had a ticket for the seat next to me looked at my legs and my trophy, then immediately asked the flight attendant if she could have another seat somewhere else on the plane. The woman simply didn't want to sit next to me. As the plane was full, she ended up sitting next to me. Her discomfort was very obvious, and for the entire three-hour flight she treated me terribly. The sad thing is she never even gave me a chance. I could have set a world record or won a Nobel Prize; if you never give anyone a chance, then you'll just never know.

Amy Palmiero-Winters is all about giving someone a chance. After all, where would she be if she hadn't been given a second one?

In 2014, Amy raised the bar a notch as she became the first athlete with a prosthesis to complete the Ultraman Triathlon. She completed the three-day race in Florida in 33:44:09.

The event included a 6.2-mile swim and a 90-mile bicycle ride on the first day, a 170-mile bicycle ride on the second day, and a 52.4-mile run on the third day.

Only 29 athletes finished the race.

RUNNING TO **EXTREMES**

CHAPTER 4

DEAN KARNAZES

"I do a lot of marathons as training runs. If I'm somewhere and there's a marathon, I'll sign up and just go run it."

I didn't say this, but I could have. Since running my first marathon in 2003, I've gone on to run 140, including one in less than four hours, in all 50 states. There are several more on the calendar. One of my favorites was the one I ran with Dean Karnazes. Although it was about eight years ago, I still enjoy vivid images and memories. One reason the memories are so clear is the film Dean's friend, JB, made of our run, included in his movie 'Ultramarathon Man: 50 Marathons, 50 States, 50 Days.' It helps that we ran the Deadwood Mickelson Trail Marathon (DMTM) course. Set in the hills of western South Dakota, the DMTM covers an old rails-to-trails route. We were blessed with a perfect autumn day—lots of bright sun illuminating the brilliant golds of the aspens and lindens and enough warmth for shorts and light shirts. Dean even donned yellow shorts.

It's not just the film, however; Dean is disarming. As you probably know, the 50 in 50 tour involved a small entourage, a large tour bus, and some amount of hype. This isn't all bad. Since we ran the course on a weekday, it was only the two of us; we had porta potties and aid stations all along the course just for us. And because it was so early on in the tour, we were pretty much alone for most of the run. Spend the better part of 26.2 miles with someone one on one, and you get a pretty good sense of whom they are. And Dean is a runner I would definitely run with again.

We had fun. We talked about all the things runners talk about—yes, everything…including bathroom issues. (In spite of the aforementioned porta potties, I had to run some interference at one point so Dean could use a bush and be assured it wouldn't end up on JB's film.) We bellyached about the course. It's a gorgeous run, but we're runners; who doesn't find something to criticize for at least one mile? This one does

RUNNING TO **EXTREMES**

go slightly uphill for the first half, so by mile 10 or 11, you're looking beyond the beauty of your surroundings, hoping to hit the promised downhill as soon as possible.

Of course, Dean is a running celebrity. I've seen how he draws a crowd. He was the featured runner and host one of the times I ran the San Francisco Marathon, and he's been on television. He has presence, good looks (one of the school girls who came out to the DMTM run asked me if he was model), and fans. Though I went into our run knowing all of this, it soon fell away, and we were just...runners. In every true sense of the word, Dean is, first and foremost, a runner. OK, let's be honest, he's a running fool. I love that about him. Anyone I can point to who helps me look a little saner and balanced in terms of how much I run is on my short list of friends. And I'd be happy to call him a friend. He's funny, self-deprecating (yes, really; he is actually quick to laugh at himself), and a good listener. He asked me as many questions as I asked him, and since I'm a trained questioner, that's saying a lot.

One of the things so very important to Dean is inspiring others, no matter how hokey that sounds. He's quite sincere about it, and he should be. He really does get people running and running distances. In May of 2014, when I was signing on to crew for Chris Roman, an endurance runner of some renown, I discovered that Chris was in another one of Dean's 50 endurance runs in 2006 (in Kentucky). Chris attributes Dean with encouraging him to go beyond the marathon distance, and did he ever! Chris has since run Badwater twice (at least once with Dean), the Leadville 100, the Keys 100, and set the American record in the Brazil 135 in 2014.

There are countless other folks who look at Dean as the person who got them up off the couch and into a pair of running shoes. Just lending out my copy of the 50 in 50 video has resulted in people telling me a friend or family member watched it with them and became determined to get moving. I've met some of them; they're regular folks who saw or felt Dean's passion and wanted to experience the joy of running for themselves.

From the little bit of time I spent with Dean and from what he's written about himself, I think it's safe to say it's not about the medals or the accolades for him. I'm guessing he'd say it's about the things running teaches you about yourself. He would focus on the process of striving, hurting, continuing, and finishing. And doing it again the next day. Maybe slower, or maybe longer, with a running buddy or alone, but doing it. My hope for him is the same as what I hope for myself and all my running buddies—that we never have to stop running.

–Amy Yanni

RUNNING TO **EXTREMES**

LIFE BEGINS (ANEW) AT 30

By Craig Snapp

When it comes to entering the world of ultramarathoning, Dean Karnazes was (as they say) late to the party. Well, actually he entered that world at the tail end *of* a party. It was the party for his 30th birthday, and that is when he decided to try to match his age by running it in years—and succeeded. At the beginning of this impromptu venture he might have been under the influence of some spirits. Afterward, the influence he was under was the Spirit of the Ultra.

(Full disclosure: "My name is Craig"..."*Hello, Craig!*"..."and I'm a Serial Marathoner." That's what I say at each week's meeting before we recite the Twelve Steps to Recovery. However, *my* malady is minor. I'm a lowercase "m" marathoner, whereas Dean is the all-caps SUPER-UBER-ULTRA-MARATHON MAN. I'm a puny portion of pâté, whereas Dean is the whole golden goose. As a runner who's never done an ultra famously said, "Anyone who does an ultramarathon is several channels short of the basic cable package!")

Dean got serious about testing his limits when he was 11. That year he completed a rim-to-rim hike of the Grand Canyon. Then he climbed Mount Whitney (a site that he would be revisiting, albeit in a slightly different manner, many times about a quarter of a century later).

At 12, he began running for his junior high school and continued when he started high school. At 14, there was a fundraiser with sponsors pledging money for each lap run around a quarter-mile track. He did 105 laps (obviously, 26-1/4 miles), which just happens to be 55 yards beyond a marathon. Technically it was his first ultramarathon.

At 15, he had some minor disagreements with his coaching staff and decided to take a brief break from running. That hiatus would last for 15 years. So as a 30-year-old he was entering a new universe with the wisdom and patience that comes with age. Therefore, he could progress at a logical, reasonable, gradual rate. Right! Apparently, he knows the line "nothing exceeds like excess," because if one is looking for logical, reasonable, and gradual in running long distances? Well, that ain't the name of this tune!

Following are just a very few of the many times Dean went to the extreme and pushed the limits of human endurance.

The Badwater Ultramarathon covers 135 miles and has been called the toughest footrace on the planet by many who should know—*those who have been there!* It begins in a spot called Badwater (282 feet below sea level—the lowest point in the contiguous states), traverses through Death Valley, and finishes at Whitney Portal (8,360 feet above sea level), which is the beginning of the trail up to the top of Mount Whitney (the highest point in the great forty-eight). Badwater veteran Scott Ludwig described the locale as "a few degrees from hell" and wrote a book bearing that title! It's possible that "few" is even an exaggeration. It may very well be less than one degree.

Logical folks might think that an event with a course description that includes the words "bad" and "death" is trying to tell us "something evil this way awaits!" Naturally, Dean has done it many times, winning once and finishing in the top 10 seven other times! He was asked what was the most important key to success: "Hmm...that's a good question. I've completed the race now 10 times and still haven't cracked that nut. When you figure it out, let me know." That was the answer, followed by almost eerie laughter. Dean should know.

RUNNING TO EXTREMES

The race is held in the dead (another ominous word) of summer, with temperatures at the mid-morning start usually in the 120s and sometimes reaching a peak to match the distance of 135! Dean was asked what he told his brain about the weather: "At Badwater, it tells you to get the hell outta there, fast! I've never said I won the race; instead I say that I survived the fastest. In many ways, Badwater is more about survival than racing."

In the year of Dean's win—rather, the year he was the fastest survivor—he had an interesting challenge. Badwater employs a wave start, and his group started four hours after the first. The last 13 miles are a "hell-acious" series of switchbacks that seem to go up, up, and then up some more, almost as if it were the stairway to heaven! (When he was questioned whether he agreed with this assessment, he commented, "It all depends on how you're feeling. Sometimes, it feels like the highway to hell.") He started that section two hours and two minutes behind the leader, who'd started the race two hours ahead of him. So there was no human target to focus on, no figure to shadow, and no physical body to catch for a side-by-side, mano-a-mano. His margin of victory was, relatively speaking, a very close seven minutes!

Marathons are a wonderful challenge and should make any finisher proud. However, if one is in the ultra world (or, as a rare few appear to be, in the super-uber-ultra world), something needs to be done with this distance to make it special. Perhaps doing 50 of them. In all 50 states. On 50 consecutive days.

At the beginning of his 50-in-triplicate trip, Dean weighed in at 154 pounds. At the end, he ended up a mere pound lighter. His last marathon was in New York City, where there's probably more television coverage worldwide than any other race. He felt that if the fatigue of the previous 49 marathons in 49 days were causing any fatigue, there would be a more-than-adequate audience to bear witness. Sorry—it didn't happen; Dean responded with his fastest marathon of those 50: 3:00:30, a pace of 6:53 per mile!

Obviously, there aren't marathons held every day. So Dean had to make arrangements to run officially measured and certified marathon courses for 42 of the days. On each of them he would run with others, ranging in number from one (for example, with Amy Yanni, who wrote Dean's introduction) to as many as a few hundred. There weren't exactly a multitude of spectators on the sidelines cheering on the efforts. There weren't exactly bands every mile, on the mile, playing *Born to Run* or *The Long Run*. It was simply a working man's version of doing 26.2. And if anyone had asked, he could have answered, "Golly, I haven't run a marathon since yesterday, and I won't run another one till tomorrow."

When asked how long it took to set up his Magical Maniacal Tour, he answered, "About two-and-a-half years of planning. I wanted to make sure that others could run along with me at the various marathons, and to do this properly required pulling all of the necessary permits and authorizations from local municipalities. We wanted to make sure we did things right and followed the sanctioned certified course."

When asked if he ever had any doubts of faith during those 50 days, he replied, "After running the Maui Marathon—in very hot and humid conditions—we took a redeye to Arizona, where the temperatures soared to nearly 100 degrees Fahrenheit. I only slept an hour that night, and by the midway point of the Arizona Marathon I was semi-delirious. That was race number 19, and I thought, 'How am I possibly going to run another 31 marathons in 31 days?' At that point, I stopped counting and just made the commitment to be the best Dean that Dean can be. Each and every morning from there on out, I got up from bed and said to myself, 'Today, I'm going to be my best; today, I'm going to try my hardest; today, I'm going to leave it all out on the course.' I just took baby steps. That's how I got through it."

There's a world record for the longest nonstop run. What *nonstop* really means is non-sleep. You can stop any time you want for as long as you want. Yet while stopped, obviously, you are not adding any distance, and more importantly, you are getting closer to Mister Sandman's ultimate shutdown time. Dean covered 350 miles in a little over 80 hours, which is a pace of 13:50 per mile! (His all-out effort defined the phrase, "pulling out all the stops.")

The first (not quite) 300 miles were done on GPS-measured roads with a support van behind him. At that point, he became mildly concerned with being light-headed and, therefore, posing a hazard to other traffic. So he asked if there was a track nearby. A map was consulted, a track was found, and he (light-) headed there.

Although he had already broken the record when he reached the track, his goal had been to finish 350 miles, so he wanted to do 50 miles more. A mere 200 loops more. The word "loop," as the base of the word "loopy" became appropriate the farther he went.

Let us simply say that this is the kind of phenomena that folks describe experiencing when they are close to ringing heaven's doorbell. Fortunately for Dean, if he was ringing, no one bothered to answer.

To the question of how he handled the sleep deprivation, he offered, 'I didn't. On the third night of sleepless running, I found myself in the middle of the road. Of course, I knew better than to run down the middle of the road, so I meandered back over to the shoulder and kept running. Before I knew it, I found myself running down the middle of the road again. That's when I realized I was running in my sleep."

Dean was asked when he decided that 350 miles would definitely serve as his finish-line tape. He answered, "When I started having out-of-body occurrences. There was a TV helicopter filming me, and I started viewing a runner from the point of view of a helicopter up in the sky, looking down at someone running along the highway. Then it flashed upon me that the person down below was, well, me."

The Golden Gate Relay is a 199-mile race from Calistoga to Santa Cruz, intended for teams consisting of 12 runners. The Dean Team did it 11 people short; in other words, as a relay of one. Eleven times, in fact. And counting! One advantage is that when Dean arrives at the relay transition point, there's no time lost in the transference of the baton. One disadvantage is that if Dean is going through a bad patch because of tired legs or any of a multitude of possible signs of fatigue, there is no runner up ahead with fresh legs to relieve him.

The Western States Endurance Run is a 100-mile race that goes through mountains and valleys, cold and heat, snow and dirt, and is arguably one of the toughest runs in the country. If runners are able to complete all 100 miles in less than 24 hours, they earn a much-coveted belt buckle. Dean has 12 belts in his wardrobe thusly buckled! One of those 12 is for the first Winter Western States Endurance Run. (That buckle has snow on the mountains!) Using a GPS, Dean and friends were able to follow the trail of the traditional race held during the summer. Dean was joined by Tim Twietmeyer (who has the distinction of the most Western States finishes), Bill Finkbeiner (most Leadville 100-mile finishes), and Jim Northey (another renowned ultramarathoner).

Dean was asked how much of the success of any performance comes from between the ears, and he referenced this one in his response: "Western States requires you to run the first 50 miles with your legs and the last 50 miles with your mind. I think that about sums it up."

RUNNING TO **EXTREMES**

When 26.2-, 30-, 100-, 135-, 199-, and 350-mile adventures have all been tackled, conquered, and enjoyed (all but the latter, much more than once), naturally one has to find a challenge of a greater distance. Such as, oh say, I don't know, 3,370 miles! Dean was invited on national television during *LIVE with Regis and Kelly* to attempt a run from Disneyland to New York City. Dean decided to attempt to run from Disneyland to New York City—from the Happiest Place on Earth to the City that Never Sleeps. (One pundit opined, "I find it appropriate that this Quest is going to begin in the home of Goofy!") He stopped at 15 schools along the way and raised over $200,000 for Action for Healthy Kids. He was invited to be the first person, literally, to run through the White House and had the opportunity to meet with Michelle Obama. He completed his own version of an Adventureland ride in 75 day, for a miles-per-day average of a fun 45!

There are 262 other stories of Dean Karnazes in his personal pushing contest against human endurance, and Dean appears to be out in front 262 to 0. I'm betting my favorite of all of my many stuffed Goofy dolls that this trend continues.

As the story goes, one day an ultramarathoner will face the Judge in the Sky. The latter will say, "You have been charged with subjecting yourself to an excessive amount of excess."

Dean Karnazes, guilty as charged.

Postscript: Dean Karnazes continues chasing dreams. His next ambition is to run a marathon in every country of the world in a one-year timespan. There are 198 countries, and he's working with the United Nations and the U.S. Department of State to make his dream a reality.

If anyone is interested in joining him, Dean says to pick a country!

DEAN KARNAZES

RUNNING TO EXTREMES

CHAPTER 5

MARK COVERT

I can remember the day I met Mark Covert. In September 1968, I went to LA Valley College to enroll in fall classes. I saw this guy in line with a crew cut, a Fu-Manchu moustache, and he was wearing dark sunglasses indoors. I thought, "Who is this guy?" A few hours later, I showed up for my first cross-country workout ever, and there he was again.

MARK COVERT

He dominated the workouts we had with Laszlo Tabori—the great Hungarian Olympian, world record holder, third man under 4:00 in the mile, and our coach. I loved Mark's tenacity, dedication, and toughness.

"Tough" is the way everybody describes Mark. Everybody!

I clung to him like a magnet. As I learned our sport and tried desperately to improve, I looked at Mark's butt for two years. Most of the time, I watched it disappear as he ran faster than I could imagine. He inspired me.

I didn't run in high school. I played baseball and was a starting pitcher on LAVC's baseball team while I tried this running thing. I loved that you could practice running on your own and didn't need anybody else. That gave me chase. As a sophomore, Mark said, "If Jon pissed me off last year, it would take me a lap to dump him. Now it takes five laps!" Hey, I was making progress thanks to training with Mark and being coached by Laszlo.

My family moved to Las Vegas in June 1969, and I got to spend a summer in hell. I was desperate to run as many miles as I could every day to catch up with all the great runners who ran in high school. That summer, I tried to duplicate what Mark had done in the summer of 1968 to make the big leap forward.

I was a big letter writer, and I told Mark how much I was running. He approved and mentioned that he'd run every day for a year, and that struck a chord with me. Wow, who does that? I asked him, "Did you run on Christmas, New Year's Day, your birthday?"

RUNNING TO **EXTREMES**

His answer was in the affirmative, and I thought, "I'm going to do that!" I'd recovered from a horrible stress fracture and shin splints and was running strong. I told Mark, "I'm going for it!"

I did it—made my year—and thought it was a nice accomplishment but not worthy of much attention. We all read about Ron Hill who had run every day for five years. I kept at it and saw how Mark was celebrated, and I became the sidebar to many of the articles that ran through the years—5 to 45 years!

I've been to every one of Mark's celebrations to honor him. When I heard he would end his streak at 45 years, I was shocked. I thought it would take a stretcher to get Mark off course. I thought back to a Japanese reporter who once rudely asked me, "Don't you want Mark's streak to end so you can be number one?"

"Are you serious? Mark is a great friend! I love the guy. I hope he runs forever!"

Mark Covert—Thanks! You are as good as they come!

—Jon Sutherland

THE LONG RUN

By Scott Ludwig

On July 24, 2013, Mark Covert did something he hadn't done in 45 years: He didn't run.

This was written several months prior to that (non-)eventful day.

1968. What a tragic, amazing, and wonderful year.

1968 was a year marred by tragedy. Martin Luther King, Jr. was assassinated. American soldiers massacred 347 civilians at Mỹ Lai. North Korea seized the U.S. Navy ship *Pueblo* and held the 83 on board as spies. Robert F. Kennedy was assassinated after winning the California primary.

1968 was a golden year for sports. The Detroit Tigers defeat the St. Louis Cardinals in a thrilling seven-game World Series. The Montreal Canadians claimed another Stanley Cup. The Green Bay Packers defended their NFL Championship by defeating the Oakland Raiders in the second Super Bowl. The Boston Celtics beat the Los Angeles Lakers in a memorable NBA Championship Series.

In 1968, the television show *60 Minutes* debuted on CBS. *Hair* opened on Broadway. *2001: A Space Odyssey* ruled the box office. *Hey Jude* topped the Billboard charts.

In 1968, U.S. unemployment was at 3.8%. The cost of a first-class stamp was $0.06. The U.S. population hovered slightly above 200 million. The average life expectancy was just over 70 years.

RUNNING TO EXTREMES

And on July 23, 1968, 17-year-old high school student Mark Covert went out for a run near his home in the suburbs of Los Angeles. There was nothing spectacular about that particular run, except for the fact that Mark would run again not only the next day and the day after that; he would run every day for the next 16,000 days, accumulating over 158,000 miles in the process. He also happens to have the longest consecutive-days running streak in the United States.

Running Becomes Second Nature

So, Mark Covert, how did running turn into such a *habit?*

"When I was in high school, I was just another high school runner. I wasn't all that special. I ran a 4:26-mile and 9:27-two-mile pace, and I wanted to be better than that. The guys in my era—back in the Stone Age that included Ron Hill, Gerry Lindgren, Ron Clark, Derrick Clayton, and Dave Bedford—they were all big mileage guys, and they always talked about running to just about anything and anywhere. So when I left high school, I had to be more consistent about running considerable mileage, which I was."

"Actually the streak started me. I was in my freshman year and noticed I had 100 days of running in a row, and I wondered if I could do it for a year. I got to one year, then three, then five...all the way up to where I am today. It wasn't something I originally set out to do; it just kind of came about. After a year of running every day, my running got so much better; the streak became a part of me. I wasn't the most talented, but if training a little bit harder would make me a bit tougher, I was all for it. I feel running every day made me tougher and smarter, which I believed was a really good reason to keep the streak going."

Running Tough

During high school, Mark was running 40 to 50 miles a week, occasionally hitting 60 and, once in a blue moon, 70. But Mark was fixated on the high-mileage runners who were regularly running 20 miles a day or more. Running three times a day was not uncommon for them.

So after graduating from high school, Mark upped his mileage to mirror the "big dogs" and ran 20 miles a day, 140 miles a week. In fact, in July of 1968, over the first 13 days of his streak, he ran 30 miles a day. On some of the days, he was just getting through the runs to work on his toughness. During his freshman year at Los Angeles Valley College, Mark's running coach was Laszlo Tabori, a man Mark refers to as "a walking, breathing legend." The facts back up Mark's contention. Tabori finished fourth in the 1500 meters and sixth in the 5000 meters in the 1960 Rome Olympics and was the world record holder at one time for the distance. He was part of the Hungarian contingent that held all the world records at one time, all the way from 1500 to 10,000 meters. Tabori was also the third man in the world to break the four-minute barrier in the mile.

Tabori was an advocate of interval training. Mark says he thought running lots of miles was hard, but what he found especially tough was working out on the track for two and three hours, five to six days a week under Tabori's tutelage. Mark remembers the toughest workout he ever ran: 40 quarters (440 yards) in 67 seconds (each). If you're not a runner, know this: That is one *tough* workout (ask any runner you know).

Mark later attended Cal State Fullerton and did a lot of hard, intense quality running that he says made him really fast, much faster than he was in high school. He ran with a great group of runners who all ran lots of miles. His roommate, Doug Schmenk, ran a 2:15 marathon. Another teammate, Dave White, ran a 2:17. They were both, in Mark's estimation, much faster than he.

RUNNING TO EXTREMES

Going into the trials, Mark realized he wasn't the fastest runner in the field, but he thought his four years of huge mileage and intense training could possibly put him in position to finish in the top three spots, earning him a spot on the U.S. Olympic team.

As every runner knows, race-day performance is everything, and on the day of the 1972 Olympic Marathon Trials, Mark Covert showed up with his A-game, hanging with the top two or three runners well into mile 21 before finishing in the seventh spot with a time of 2:23:35, a little over three minutes behind the coveted spot of the third-place finisher, Jack Bacheler.

"Because of the streak, everybody thinks of me as a great endurance athlete, says Mark. "I look at ultrarunners; they are amazing individuals. I think the idea of me being a marathoner is just not true. I only ran three or four [marathons], and dropped out of a few others. I used to like running 16 to 18 miles, but not every weekend. I used to run my workouts hard because I didn't like to be out for more than two hours."

Regardless of Mark's contention of not being a marathon runner, his best was a 2:21 at the World Master Marathon in Orange City, Florida. Some would say a 2:21 most definitely qualifies Mark as a true marathoner.

A Nike First

At the 1972 Olympic Marathon Trials, Mark had the distinction of being the first runner ever to cross a finish line in a pair of Nike running shoes. Here's the story:

Nike (originally Blue Ribbon Sports) was putting their running shoes out for the very first time. Mark wandered into a running store in Eugene,

Oregon, (where the marathon trials would be held) that was giving out free shoes and T-shirts to the athletes. Merely wanting a free T-shirt, Mark caught the eye of Jeff Hollister who was looking for runners to wear his newly designed shoes in the trials. Hollister traced the outline of Mark's feet and made a shoe with a lot of rubber studs on the bottom that created a waffle-soled look. Mark gave them a couple of test runs and told Jeff he would wear the shoes, but only if he could get another T-shirt. ("They paid big money to get me in those shoes," Mark jokes.)

"They made about eight pair, but only three or four of us actually wore them in the trials, says Mark. "I was the first guy to cross the finish line in a pair of Nike waffle shoes. I have them in a safety deposit box. I don't wear them anywhere. They only come out on rare occasions. Me and Nike have been, in some way, shape, or form, tied at the hip ever since."

In 1992, Mark was inducted into the Nike Hall of Fame.

Family Life

Mark met his wife, Debi, while he was teaching at LA Valley College. They both went to the same high school, but she was three years behind him, and they actually met while Debi was in a class Mark was teaching. They eventually shared a college class together and knew *of* one another, but it wasn't until later they actually started dating.

Mark started teaching and coaching in 1974. Initially a part-time instructor, he eventually landed a full-time job with Antelope Valley College in Lancaster, California. Mark and Debi have four children, all between the ages of 26 and 31. Quite obviously, Mark managed to squeeze in his daily run on the occasion of all four of their births. Debi jokingly refers to her husband's streak as their fifth child.

RUNNING TO EXTREMES

Debi is a runner, but she prefers to do her running inside on a treadmill. Although not a streak runner like her husband, she still gets in her morning run five or six times a week. Mark usually heads out for his run at 5:00 a.m., about the time Debi has already been on the treadmill for 30 minutes. Mark meets his team for track practice at 6 a.m., and Debi leaves the house around 6:30 a.m. The busy lives of a running couple that both work offers little time to be together.

Mark lost both of his parents to cancer. In fact, his mother had both breast and lung cancer, and after it was diagnosed, it was only a matter of three or four months before she passed away.

"She was pretty sick," Mark says. "The running made it better. When you run by yourself, there is a lot of time for reflection, thinking about things and such. My mom and dad were big supporters of everything that I did, no matter what it was. Getting out and running the day she passed and in the days leading up to the funeral—I know they would have been surprised if I didn't go out and run. Days when it's difficult, it's a good thing to go and escape for a while. On those days, it was an escape from the situation. It was important to get out on those days."

It's apparent that running for Mark Covert is therapeutic. He says, "I run most of the time by myself now. To have that time in the morning for 30 to 70 minutes just makes me feel better. It's my time of the day: to think about things like what the day has in store for me, my job, my family, my team, or whatever. It just kind of reduces the stress level and takes the pressure off for a while. When I'm done running, I just plain feel better. It's something I think makes me feel better and, in a lot of ways, makes me a better person. It helps me look at the day a little bit clearer after my run. It is really important to me."

Most nights, Mark is in bed by 9:00 p.m. Possessing a sleep disorder, he regularly is out of bed by 3:30 the next morning. To Mark, getting six hours of sleep on any given night is considered a minor victory. He wishes he could sleep eight hours, but that just hasn't been the case.

The Streak

Of course, Mark's sleeping habits lend themselves to preserving the streak. For a streak runner, the best course of action is to get the run in first thing in the morning for the reasons Mark already described as well as just in case something happens later in the day that might jeopardize the daily run. Naturally, there are days Mark doesn't feel like going out for a run, but living in a climate where there is rarely horrible weather (OK, in winter the wind chill may hit single digits, but other than that, it's California, people) makes that daily run just a little bit easier to stomach, even on the days Mark would rather be doing something else, needs to be doing something else, or simply doesn't feel well.

Mark has the longest active consecutive-days running streak in the United States as recognized by the United States Running Streak Association (USRSA). Less than one year behind him is his friend, Jon Sutherland.

Mark says, "Jon and I went to school together, so we know each other. I know Jon thinks he can go on just as I thought I could do the same. We joke about it but never really talked about it. I know he has problems with his ankles and feet, but I'm not really sure where he is health-wise. Once you get past 30 to 35 years, a couple things come into play: wear and tear, age, and things starting to multiply. The person with the longest running streak for women ended hers a while back when she slipped and broke her ankle. Ken Young tore his abdominal muscle and ended his streak not long after reaching 41.5 years. As we get older, all these things are so much different than when we are younger. When I was younger, I would get hurt and be back running in a few days; now I hope it heals in three months. It's a completely different thing. Jon and I only see each other once or twice a year. I know Jon knows about me and me a little bit about him. I don't know if he's anxious to end his streak so he can move on."

Mark's worse run might well have been in November 2012 when he was dealing with kidney stones. He was really sick and taking some particularly strong pain medication. The runs would go well, but afterwards he would experience unbelievable back spasms. Not only were the two or three runs incredibly painful, but the aftermath was even worse.

Mark also suffers from back pain, the result of his right foot being crooked, making for a twisted foot strike which results in pain in his lower back. The discomfort on his right side is somewhat painful when he runs—on cold mornings, even more so. Mark tried therapy, but until he decides to have reconstructive surgery on his foot, he is going to have to live with the back pain. "It's something I've learned to tolerate," he says. "I'm not anxious to deal with it every day, but I *can* deal with it."

In recent years, Mark has cut back on his mileage. "Not consciously; it just happened," he says. In fact, he was still running 60 to 80 miles a week (and 100 miles a week during the summer) as recently as 10 years ago. Then, as the feet problems intensified, his job required more time, and the miles didn't go by as quickly as they once had, the weekly mileage decreased. Mark has assumed an administrative position in California with the Community College Track and Field program. Mark's school just got a new track, and they are now regularly hosting large track meets. "I still try to run at least 30 miles a week, and every once in a while, I'll hit 40." (Note: After ending his streak, Mark began spending more time on the bicycle—and less time running—to maintain his fitness.)

In the speed department, Mark was still cranking out a seven-minute pace during runs of 10 to 12 miles as recently as three years ago. Today? Mark says, "I'm a 10- to 12-minute mile guy. The trees pass me by real slow now, but that's OK.' Mark's problem is that darn foot; the one he has to drag as he runs. The problem isn't that he has to run slow; it's that he can't run the way he always did: Hard. 'That's something I can't do anymore; all I can do is plug along.'

Mark adds that he still competes in races although they 'have to put a stick in the ground to use as a sundial' to time him.

Home Stretch

Anyone who has run for any length of time knows injuries are inevitable. Most runners simply take time off to nurse their wounds, recover from their surgeries or simply rest until whatever ails them goes away.

But Mark Covert is not 'most runners.'

The day after Mark broke his foot; the day after he had meniscus surgery on his knee; the day after he hurt his back, and it was hard to bend over or walk, let alone run. But he did anyway, allowing the streak to live another day.

Regarding the broken foot, specifically the fifth metatarsal on his left foot, Mark's foot was so swollen the doctors didn't want to put a full cast on it. Instead, they wrapped it and sent him home. Mark took the half cast off the following morning, wrapped his foot as tight as he possibly could, and slipped it into a construction boot, virtually immobilizing the foot in the process. He went out for a run and discovered it would suffice—albeit with quite a bit of pain for the first four or five days. A few weeks later, the pain diminished—either that or Mark had developed a tolerance for the pain or quite simply refused to acknowledge it. As long as the pain wasn't getting worse, he believed the foot was healing. The podiatrist agreed but told Mark the original estimate of recovery in six to eight weeks was now going to be 10 to 12 weeks due to the punishment he was subjecting his foot to.

As for the knee surgery, Mark says the torn meniscus was actually not as bad as you might be led to believe. The discomfort from the surgery was caused by the doctors' instruments poking around his knee and not from the meniscus tear or the actual procedure to repair the knee. The doctor's advised Mark that while he was not going to hurt himself running, he would still advise against it. "So knowing that, I knew I could go out and hobble around on it [the knee]. My wife went out with me for the first week or so and ran a mile with me every morning and kept the streak alive."

Then there was the time a couple of Novembers ago when Mark suffered from kidney stones, and he thought he might just die from the pain. He looks back on days like those and knows they were the real challenges to end his streak. But then again, Mark has always liked challenges. Mark says, "As long as I wasn't going to do any permanent damage, I didn't see any reason why I shouldn't put my shoes on and go for a run."

"I've surrounded myself with great doctors over the years who have bought into this craziness. They understood if they told me 'no' I'd go out and try to do it anyway. They would never say 'go out and try this' if it were going to cause real damage. They've really been tremendously supportive."

Then again, it helps that Mark enjoys doing what he does, each and every day. He likes putting on his running shoes, going for a run, and testing himself, pushing a little bit more every day. He says, "It [the streak] just became a part of life; like how one gets up and brushes their teeth, it's just something I do. I suppose there was a point of no return, but if there was, I didn't notice. I never thought I couldn't ever miss a day running again. It's just something I do."

All Good Things...

How long could it last?

Mark's heard that question countless times. Five or six years ago, he truly believed the streak could go on forever. But as he got older and the physical issues mounted, he came to the realization that one day the longest consecutive-days running streak in the United States might come to an end.

"I am struggling," Mark says. "I have a lot of problems with my foot and back because of the foot. Ever since I was a small kid, I had horribly flat feet, and in the last five years, they have gotten much worse. I'm told I have mid-foot collapse on my right foot. It's completely collapsed and twisted so that it points outward. The best I can say is that I hobble along, doing three to six miles at a much slower pace."

Mark admits he never had a specific goal with respect to the streak. However, he did say he wanted to celebrate the 45th anniversary of the streak. "If I live through track season with all the events I'm hosting with

RUNNING TO EXTREMES

my team, I am sure I can get to 45. After that, if it comes to an end, it comes to an end. I can live with that."

"Right now most people say I shouldn't do it [end the streak]. My doctor says I'm not harming myself, so I am going to keep doing it for a while longer. If I get to 45 [years], and I can continue doing this, I'll have to make a decision. I can't really run hard at this point, so I'm just moving along, doing 9- to 11-minute miles and shuffling around to get my runs in. I like to train hard so I'm supplementing my running with getting on the bike. I find that I enjoy the bike quite a bit. I may get to a point somewhere down the line and realize I can do better for myself on the bike and just start cranking it up on the bike for an hour-and a-half or two as opposed to shuffling around for the sake of keeping the streak alive."

To Streak or Not To Streak

Mark has these words of advice for anyone considering a running streak of their own: Don't do it.

"I have a couple of kids [on his team] who have six or seven years [of running every day] in. I don't really talk much to my team about them; I feel you need to take days off when you're sick and things like that. Occasionally, one will say they're close to eight months, and I tell them take a week off when the season comes to an end. My running career is winding down. I've been taping my foot twice a day for the past 18 months. If I just took three weeks off, it would have been better again. I think it depends on where you are in your career; if you're young, do the things that are intelligent. If you start at 35-plus years and your goals and aspirations are not being the best in the country or going to the nationals, I can see where you can say it's good for your fitness, and you're going to run every day. Maybe that's a good thing for their psychological health and well-being. Remember, this is what I was saying about running being therapeutic. Those that are young and want to race well, there are some good things in having a streak, but I promise you're doing physical harm to yourself. Especially if you have the flu, just take the time off."

Aspiring streak runners, please heed the advice of Mark Covert.

After all, he knows a thing or two about streak running.

Mark Covert would eventually end his streak exactly 45 years after it began.

A mere 307 days later, his pal from school, Jon Sutherland of West Hills, California, took over the top spot.

CHAPTER 6

BOBBI GIBB

Although it seems like yesterday, the year was 1980, and it was on a warm midsummer day in Boston that I first glimpsed a blond, willowy female, descending the steps from the street level above. As she entered the doorway leading into Bill Rodgers Running Center's basement

location, 372-A Chestnut Hill Avenue, I stood awestruck upon realizing who it was.

I was an aspiring 19-year-old runner from Texas, one of a handful of runners fortunate enough to be in the employ of the world's then number-one ranked marathoner, Bill Rodgers, and the beautiful, soft-spoken apparition standing in front of me was none other than Bobbi Gibb, Boston's "first lady."

Following that first encounter, almost three decades would lapse before I ran into Bobbi again, albeit on the other side of the country. I was living in San Diego at the time, and a neighbor mentioned he'd run into a woman at a function who had run the Boston Marathon, not to mention he was under the impression she'd gained some notoriety for her participation in the event.

Upon asking my neighbor what her name was, he remarked, "I think it was Bobbi—could that be right?" To which I responded, "Bobbi Gibb?" "Yeah, that's it!" he answered.

To that he added, "I told her you were a runner, had spent time in Boston, and knew Bill Rodgers, and she said she'd like to meet you."

Needless to say, my curiosity was piqued, but short of any contact information, I decided to email the Boston Athletic Association, tell them a bit about myself, and mention I wanted to get in touch with Bobbi. That said, courtesy of the BAA's Gloria Ratti, Bobbi and I became reacquainted in 2006.

During the years since, I feel fortunate to have shared many miles with Bobbi. She's without a doubt the embodiment of what a true runner

RUNNING TO **EXTREMES**

is given her natural passion for one of, if not the, most natural and introspective of sports.

With that in mind, as quiet and unassuming as Boston's first lady is, the expression "still waters run deep" comes to mind when I think of Bobbi Gibb.

On that note, after being interviewed extensively for the film, Spirit of the Marathon (2007), Bobbi invited me to attend a screening with her and was excited about being featured in a movie highlighting the passion of those who share her love for running.

Unfortunately, as the final credits of Spirit of the Marathon began to roll across the screen—the entire movie had been devoid of one shot or even one mention of her—Bobbi turned to me in the darkness of the theater and whispered, "Well, I guess I don't exist."

Yes, Bobbi, you do exist, and thank you for inspiring not only me but more so the countless others you paved the way for on that April day in 1966.

–Dave Dial

THE FIRST LADY OF HOPKINTON

By Scott Ludwig

I spoke with Bobbi-Lou (as she was known growing up) for the first time on May 25, 2008. A mutual friend had introduced us several days earlier in a 21st-century kind of way: email. Our first conversation was more 20th-century as we communicated by more conventional methods: over the telephone. I'm glad we opted for the give-and-take of an actual conversation, because I would have hated it if Bobbi-Lou's enthusiasm and love for the sport of running had been lost in translation had I simply read her written words. Her motivation is simple: *"I just love to run."* No truer words were ever spoken. When she told me that in her world, running is a spiritual experience, the sincerity and enthusiasm in her voice during our 90-minute conversation made me realize that Bobbi-Lou has the purest love for the sport of anyone I have ever met.

Most of you know Bobbi-Lou as Roberta Louise Gibb, recognized by the Boston Athletic Association (BAA) as the first woman to complete the Boston marathon. Bobbi, the name most of us know her by, accomplished this feat in 1966—six years before women were officially allowed to enter the most prestigious marathon in the world. Prior to 1972, it was common "knowledge" that women were physiologically unable to run distances greater than 1.5 miles. However, Bobbi's training runs—which would have been legendary had they been known—quite frequently were of distances between 30 and 40 miles. She knew in her heart that she had what it took to complete the Boston Marathon, a race she first watched and fell in love with in 1964.

RUNNING TO EXTREMES

The Long Road to Hopkinton

Bobbi knew the instant she watched her first Boston Marathon that one day she wanted to traverse the 26.2-mile route from Hopkinton to Boston. She trained fiercely for two years, running through the fields and mountains of the U.S. with an assortment of neighborhood dogs that served as her friends and protectors during her long hours on the trails. In the mid-1960s, there were no women's running shoes, so she opted to run in nurses' shoes. There were also no training books on running, so everything Bobbi learned was through firsthand experience.

Bobbi discovered a fondness for long training runs. Many days, she and her boyfriend would go on motorcycle rides, and on the way home, Bobbi would ask to be dropped off along the way so she could run home. She traveled across the country in 1964 and used the experience to complete long training runs (with Moot, a white malamute) in various cities along the way. When she arrived on the west coast, she still did not realize *how* long her runs were until meeting a local running hero. Bill Gookin noticed Bobbi's running prowess and asked about her routes; he quickly calculated that she was regularly covering distances of 25 miles or more. But Bobbi was not concerned with distance; after all, she just loved to run.

In 1965, Bobbi considered running Boston, but injuries to both her ankles postponed her hopes for another year. She attended Tufts University during the day and worked as a nanny at night, all the while maintaining her training regimen for the day when she would finally make her initial appearance in Hopkinton. In the fall of 1965, she traveled to Vermont to watch a 100-mile equestrian event. Wanting to make the best use of her time, she decided to run alongside the horses the first day of the event, covering 40 miles over rough terrain. As she entered the town of Woodstock, a spectator gave her a carrot—the same thing given to the horses. While it may have been given in a humorous vein, it was also given out of respect for what Bobbi had done: run 40 miles on a difficult course in a single day. The next day she ran another 25 miles.

Bobbi married the gentleman who introduced her to cross-country running at Tufts University in January of 1966, and they moved to San Diego, California. Three months later she would return to her home state of Massachusetts to fulfill an appointment with history.

At Long Last

Early in 1966, Bobbi wrote to Will Cloney of the BAA for an application to April's Boston Marathon. Her request resulted in more than a rejection: the now-famous response from Cloney detailed women's perceived physiological running limitations.

Officially Bobbi was refused entry as it was thought that women were not capable of running more than a mile and a half and, therefore, were not allowed to do so under AAU rules due to safety concerns. Bobbi realized this made her quest even more important as she wanted to prove that a woman could run marathon distances. She felt that once everyone knew the truth, the rules could be changed, and the Boston Marathon would allow women to enter. However, she was facing a catch-22: How could she prove something she was not allowed to do?

Undeterred, Bobbi took a three-day Greyhound bus ride back to Boston. Once she arrived in town, she called her parents and told them of her plans to run the marathon. They both thought she was nuts; in fact, her dad thought she may very well kill herself running.

On Patriot's Day (the traditional day for the running of the Boston Marathon), Bobbi's dad left the house to preside over a sailboat race.

RUNNING TO EXTREMES

Once he left the house, Bobbi asked her mom to drive her to Hopkinton. By giving Bobbi a ride, her mom also left her mark in history.

Bobbi was attired in a black bathing suit tank top, boy's size 6 running shoes, her brother's Bermuda shorts, and a blue hooded sweatshirt which she wore with the hood up to hide her long hair. The hood also covered something else: her femininity.

Bobbi arrived in Hopkinton two hours before the start of the race. Feeling a bit anxious—or was it *impatient?*—she opted to run several miles behind a row of houses before the marathon started. She then hid in the bushes to await her appointment with destiny. Once the race began, Bobbi slipped into the race somewhere near the middle of the pack. After running alongside several men for three minutes, one of the men turned to her and asked no one in particular, "Is that a girl?"

Once Bobbi made her gender known, she feared that they would force her out of the race. She even thought that she might end up in jail. After all, women were prohibited from entering this prestigious men-only event.

Fortunately, just the opposite occurred. The men thought running alongside this brave and endearing woman was great. And not a minute too soon, as the hood was making her really hot. She now felt more comfortable letting her guard down, especially since the men reassured her that they wouldn't let anything happen to her.

During the course of the race, word spread that there was a woman competing in the field. The crowd began supporting her. Radio broadcasts were fascinated with the developing story that a woman was not only *running* in the Boston Marathon, but might actually *complete* it. History was being made, and it was evident that Bobbi had captured the imagination of an entire city.

Bobbi maintained a sub-three-hour pace for most of the race, but the ill-fated and ill-fitting running shoes were taking a horrible toll on her feet. She was also becoming dehydrated, as she had not been drinking fluids along the course. In 1966, it was a popular misconception that drinking water during long-distance events caused cramps. While her pace slowed in the latter miles of the race, she found herself becoming increasingly afraid of failing. Bobbi *had* to succeed or face the possibility of personally setting women's running back decades.

Bobbi crossed the finish line 3 hours and 21 minutes after she darted out from behind the bushes in Hopkinton. She made history and provided scientific support that the so-called "weaker sex" could indeed run farther than 1.5 miles. A whole lot farther, in fact. She even beat more than half the men in the field!

While Bobbi's performance had captured the imagination of the city (and later the entire world), that was not the case with the officials of the marathon. Bobbi was denied the traditional finishers' beef stew. She was not awarded a medal. After all, she was still a woman. And women didn't have a place in this prestigious men-only event.

Bobbi took a taxi home to Winchester, only to discover that the streets were full of cars. She figured that many of the neighbors were having Patriot's Day parties. She was wrong. The cars were there to celebrate a historic event: *Little Bobbi-Lou had just finished the Boston Marathon.*

The next day, her accomplishment made front-page headlines throughout Boston and the neighboring towns. One newspaper, in an effort to portray Bobbi as feminine (even though she could run a "masculine" 26.2 miles), took pictures of her in a dress making fudge in her parents' kitchen. The next day, most of the local papers featured Bobbi's accomplishment on the front page. *Sports Illustrated* did a story on her. *Sports Illustrated!*

RUNNING TO EXTREMES

She'll Always Be the First

Bobbi ran the Boston Marathon again in 1967 and 1968. During this pre-sanctioned era, Bobbi was the first woman finisher on both occasions, extending her unofficial winning streak to three years. In 1967, she finished in front of Kathrine Switzer by over an hour. In 1968, Bobbi finished in front of the four other women in the race.

In her autobiography, Kathrine Switzer promotes herself as the first woman to officially enter and run in the Boston Marathon, one year after Bobbi's Hopkinton debut. Bobbi questions the "official" status of this endeavor since Switzer failed one of the primary qualifications to be an official Boston Marathon entry: She was not a man. Although some deception merited Switzer a race number, Switzer, like Bobbi-Lou, was a very "unofficial" participant in this legendary race. (A historical footnote: There were no official women entrants in the Boston Marathon until 1972 when the BAA created a women's division race.)

The reason Switzer has received even more attention is that by being an unqualified entrant and running with an invalid number, she posed serious accreditation issues to the Boston Marathon. Her "official" participation threatened to invalidate the finishing times of the qualified male entrants. This was the primary motivation for Jock Semple, a man whom Bobbi describes as "a great man who doesn't deserve to be misrepresented" when he made his infamous attempt to physically remove Switzer's number during the race.

But for the sake of historical accuracy, Roberta Louise Gibb will always be "the First."

Immortality

It took 30 years for the Boston Marathon to recognize Bobbi's accomplishment. In 1996, Bobbi was officially recognized by the BAA as the winner of the Boston Marathon three straight years in what is now called the pre-sanctioned era. To commemorate this accomplishment, the BAA presented her with a medal emblazoned with those three memorable years: 1966, 1967, and 1968.

As importantly, Bobbi Gibb's name has been permanently engraved on the Boston Marathon memorial in Copley Square, an enduring tribute to the First Lady of Hopkinton.

Lasting Impression

In the short time I have known her, I have found Bobbi to be a woman who is not only generous with her time, but is also generous in bearing her soul. To hear her speak—for an hour, for a minute, *for just a few seconds*—is to hear the words of someone who absolutely cherishes the freedom to run through the fields and mountains in the company of her four-legged companions. She epitomizes—truly—the spirit of running.

Roberta Louise Gibb was the first woman to finish the Boston Marathon. There will never be another like her, and I am proud to have this opportunity to tell her story—to pass on a piece of history that bears telling time after time.

Postscript: While it's been 50-plus years since Bobbi's first Boston effort, her love for running remains unwavering.

Now in her 70s, she continues to run for an hour or more each day.

RUNNING TO **EXTREMES**

CHAPTER 7

MIKE MORTON

MIKE MORTON

I will never forget the story Eric Clifton once told me about one of his race experiences at the 40-mile Uwharrie Mountain Run in North Carolina. Eric won the first Uwharrie, and I won it the second year. Several years after that, Eric was running the race and running very well. The Uwharrie 40-miler is a course that goes 20 miles out from the start and then turns around and comes back the same twisty single-track course. All the way out to 20 miles, Eric was running record splits. He thought he should be blowing the field away, but he said this young kid *just stayed on his shoulder. All the way back, he said he kept running fast and was setting record splits, yet the* kid *stayed on his shoulder. Finally, with a few miles to go, he pulled away from the* kid *and set a course record, beating the* kid *by just a couple of minutes. The name of the* kid? *Mike Morton, running in his first ultra.*

Back in the 90s, I was training a good friend of mine, Donald Smith. He was getting in good shape and placing in the top five of most ultras but had not won his first race. He told me about a new 50-mile race that had just started in Eastern Virginia. I told him that he should go there and win his first ultra. He went, ran very well, and got second place. I asked him who beat him and, he said some young baby-faced kid. *What was the* kid's *name?* Mike Morton *winning his first ultra.*

Even in the early days of his ultra career, Mike was very competitive.

–David Horton

RUNNING TO EXTREMES

EVEN BETTER THE SECOND TIME AROUND

By Scott Ludwig

Quick Study

Mike Morton started running while he was in high school. Up until high school, the only sport he ever played was football: peewee, junior high school, and finally high school. Ever the short, heavy kid, that all began to change one summer when his older brother (there were four others) came home from the Navy for a visit and suggested Mike start getting in shape for football camp. The two of them went out for a 3.2-mile run that made the proverbial light bulb go off in Mike's head, enlightening him to the overwhelming belief that he was *supposed* to be running. He didn't want to stop.

Mike ran track during his last two years of high school after quitting the football team. He never gave any thought to a potential college scholarship for running, only because he was oblivious to how fast he was. Here he was doing 6-minute miles in his training runs, but to Mike that was just normal—at least until he started competing and found that his pace was anything but normal. (His 3200-meter PR in high school was 10:30!) Although never being competitive at the state level, he was high in the pecking order of his part of the state. He had also read about Ann Trason during his senior year and knew one day he—like Ann Trason—would run 100-mile races.

Mike, reflecting on the hour-and-a-half bus ride to and from school, had this to say: "It was 13 miles, and I started doing the math. I was thinking I could run home faster than the bus takes to get me there. So I started running home only to hear people tell me it wasn't normal for people to run that far every day. I was thinking I was simply killing two birds with one stone: I could get a run in, and I was getting home from school before my brothers."

Act One: Farther and Faster

Mike started running ultramarathons in 1994. After a debut at the 40-mile Uwharrie Mountain Run in North Carolina, he quickly upped the ante to 50 miles, and before long he was running 100 miles at a clip. And what a clip it was. His first foray into the 100-mile distance signaled his arrival: a victory at Old Dominion in 17 hours and 40 minutes. There was, indeed, a new sheriff in town.

After a 100-mile debut like that, what did Mike do for an encore? How about lowering his time by 45 minutes at Old Dominion the very next year, winning for the second time in a row. Or lowering that time by (hold on to your hats) *2 hours and 47 minutes* at the 1995 Vermont 100, winning in a sprint-like 14 hours and 8 minutes. In other words, Mike ran 100 miles at an overall pace of 8 minutes and 29 seconds per mile.

Which brings us to 1996. Mike wins the Massanutten Mountain Trails 100-Mile Run in his debut in 20 hours and 21 minutes, setting the stage for his Western States Endurance Run debut that same year. Up until this point, Mike had been running primarily on the east coast as it was too expensive to be going running all over the country. But now it was time for Mike to truly make his name a household word.

But Mike's first time out in the mountains of the Sierra Nevada didn't turn out so well. He got lost around mile 45 and guesses that he and his running partner, Courtney Campbell, both lost about 40 minutes or more. Mike was running in third place at the time, but when he found his way back onto the course, he had dropped 14 spots in the standings. He gave it everything he had to make up for lost time, but once he got to the bank of the Rucky Chucky River crossing at 78 miles, he lost his momentum when he was forced to wait 20 minutes to be transported by paddleboat to the other side. Mike ultimately dropped out of the race after 85 miles.

Mike returned to Western States in 1997, intent on correcting what in his book was a terrible wrong. And correct it he did, winning arguably the most prestigious ultramarathon in the country in a record time of 15 hours and 40 minutes, finishing an astounding 93 minutes in front of second-place finisher (and Western States legend), Tim Twietmeyer. Mike also became the first non-Californian to win the event and bettered the existing course record by just over 13 minutes.

Disappearing Act

After 1997, Mike began having hip problems. He says, "I fell that winter, and it jacked up my hip and knee and progressively worsened. After Western, I ran a couple of races, including the Rattlesnake 50K and a four-day stage race on trails across the commonwealth." During the latter, Mike competed and won against two legends of the sport: Eric Clifton and David Horton. It would be his last victory of the century before the pain in his hip got the best of him. He had surgery in February of 1998 but was feeling devastated not being able to run at full strength. Beyond that, he doubted his commitment to running, feeling a bit immature for putting it as the focal point of his life.

Mike initially was a diver in the Navy, having enlisted right after graduating from high school. Navy life took him to Puerto Rico until one day in 2000, when the Army came recruiting, looking for men to switch to Special Forces. They found their man in Mike; it wasn't long before he became a Green Beret. The next year, Mike began training, and then it happened. "It," as in 9/11. Once the war started, Mike had tours in both Iraq and Afghanistan, leaving very little time for running.

From 2003 to 2010, Mike would serve in Iraq for four or five months at a time with a 10-month break at home sandwiched between. He would also do two five-month hitches in Afghanistan. In 2003, Mike began a relationship with Julie, who he would marry in 2008. Mike and Julie have a daughter named Bailey, who proud dad refers to as "the most perfect kid in the world."

All in all, it would be another 12 years before Mike and ultrarunning resumed their torrid affair.

Mike was sitting in Afghanistan in 2010 with some friends when it dawned on him: There was still a competitive fire burning inside of him. He began training; he was refocused. It wouldn't be long before that competitive fire would be burning up the ultrarunning community once again.

Act Two: Even Farther and Faster

So after seven years spent protecting our country in the most hostile environments on the planet, Mike focused his attention on his imminent return to the sport he loved most. He circled the 2010 Hinson Lake 24-Hour Run in North Carolina on his calendar and immediately began increasing his training mileage. To no one's surprise except perhaps his own, Mike won the event by completing almost 154 miles on a 1.52-mile trail loop.

Mike returned to Hinson Lake the following year and ran 10 miles farther, running almost 164 miles in 90-degree heat while encountering the occasional course congestion throughout the day (and night). His performance was less than two miles shy of the American record held by Scott Jurek, established on a flat course with a smooth surface.

RUNNING TO EXTREMES

By the time 2012 rolled around, Mike was poised to re-establish himself among the elite. It didn't take long. Before Memorial Day rolled around, Mike was victorious in three 100-mile races. He completed all of them in less than 14 hours:

January 21, 2012—Long Haul 100-Mile Run. Finish time: 13:18:58.

March 31, 2012—Umstead 100-Mile Endurance Run. Finish time: 13:11:40.

May 19, 2012—Keys Ultra 100-Mile Run. Finish time: 13:42:52.

The sheriff was back in town.

It should come as no surprise, then, that Mike would ultimately be recognized as the 2012 North American Ultramarathon Runner of the Year by *Ultrarunning* magazine. Or that his three 100-mile victories were just the beginning. The best was yet to come.

Mike had a special affinity for the Badwater Ultramarathon, as his good friend Eric Clifton had run it three times and through their many shared training miles together came to become very familiar with the contours and challenges of the 135-mile course. Mike saw Badwater as having an atmosphere of its own, and the challenges of the weather helped to make it a rather unique event. "It's not like your typical 100, where you can fight through it," Mike says. "There is just so much there that you can't plan for; it's amazing."

Amazing. That pretty much describes Mike's performance as he made his way across Death Valley and ultimately reached the finish line at the Portals of Mount Whitney. Mike says, "It became one of those races where everything went great. I don't have any regrets." Outside of a nagging stomach problem during the night—resulting in no fewer than seven trips to the bathroom—there was little Mike could have improved upon. Except...

"At one point when the sun came up, for some reason, I wanted to change my shorts. So I crossed the road and started searching in the van. And I know I spent over a minute digging through my bag but never found them. So I said #*$& it. I don't have time to stand here. I'm just going to keep running."

Mike won the race by almost 40 minutes, finishing in 22:52:55. His finishing time was only 86 seconds slower than the course record established by Valmir Nunes in 2007. Eighty-six seconds, or as Mike remembers it, approximately the amount of time he spent searching for his phantom pair of shorts.

Less than three months after Badwater, Mike competed in the 24-Hour Run World Championship in Kalowice, Poland. It's doubtful he wasted another 86 seconds this time around, as he ran a phenomenal 172.4 miles—easily outdistancing the second-place runner who finished more than 10 miles behind Mike's blistering pace. Mike established a new U.S. record in the process—almost seven miles farther than the previous record of 165.7 miles set three years prior by none other than Scott Jurek. It's also worth mentioning Mike eclipsed the 100-mile barrier after a mere 13 hours and 10 minutes had elapsed off the clock.

"At the World 24-Hour you could feel the tension; everybody there was competitive. It was the top runners from every country; you could feel it when you talked to people. It felt like everyone had their eyes glued on you, so it created a very energetic atmosphere for me the entire time. Seeing the Japanese guys, in the middle of the night, knowing I was six miles ahead of them, it motivated me. It was very unique. I had one of those days where nothing went wrong, nothing bothered me, and I was on autopilot. I truly believe I ran too conservatively early in the race; I was so focused on the 50-mile, 100-mile, and 21-hour splits and hitting those targets. I wanted to make sure of getting the American record; I didn't want to run for 23 hours and miss the record again by such a small margin. I just ran based on my perceived effort level and was able to step it up." Spoken like a true champion, as well as a U.S. record holder in the 24-hour run, the first American male to ever win a World Championship Ultra distance event, and the US Track & Field Ultra Runner of the Year.

In the winter of 2013, Mike won two 100-mile events: Iron Horse (13:14) and Rocky Raccoon (14:28). At Rocky Raccoon, Mike admitted running a terrible race and wanted to drop out after 40 miles, but he was told he had a 40-minute lead, so he kept running and finished 94 minutes ahead of the second finisher. (At Iron Horse, Mike only won by a mere 84 minutes.) Perhaps the most impressive thing about Mike's back-to-back victories is that they occurred on back-to-back Saturdays in February.

During the summer of 2013, Mike returned to California to test his belief that he was now a stronger runner at 41 than he was the first time around at age 25—not necessarily faster but certainly more mature. He attributes his mental strength to his service with the military. "Without a doubt, just the maturity, dealing with things when they're not going good," says Mike. There isn't an ultrarunner alive who hasn't had to deal with things when they're not doing well; as talented as he is, Mike is no exception to this tried and true fact of the sport.

At the age of 41 — 16 years after his win at Western Statues as a 25-year-old — Mike ran the 100.2 miles from Squaw Valley to Auburn a mere five minutes slower than his winning time in 1997. The performance placed him third overall, but more importantly it earned him a victory among male masters runners; the second place male master finished almost two hours after Mike.

Act Three: The Best Is Yet to Come

Mike looks back to 1997 when he was the first non-Californian to win the Western States Endurance Run, breaking the course record in the process and failing to get any recognition.

Today, a humbled Mike admits being named the 2012 North American Ultrarunner of the Year by his peers is the crowning achievement of his life forever.

A profound statement when these impressive credentials are taken into consideration:

A marathon best of 2:36 (5:56 per mile pace)

A 50-mile best of 5:42 (6:50 per mile pace)

A 100-mile best of 13:10 (7:54 per mile pace)

A 24-hour best of 172.45 miles (8:21 per mile pace)

But these may be just the beginning. Mike knows the road record for a 24-hour run on roads is 180 miles. He says, "I think a couple of guys are right on the cusp [of breaking the record]. If you have the right day, the right weather, 178 to 180 miles is within the realm of possibility with the right approach, the right game plan, and the right efficiency."

There is a video of the 2012 Badwater Ultramarathon, showing Mike running in the mountains during the night when race director, Chris Kostman, pulls up alongside in a car and asks him what his strategy will be for the miles ahead. Without missing a beat, Mike, looking straight ahead and eyes focused clearly on the prize simply says,

Keep running.
What else would you have expected him to say?

RUNNING TO **EXTREMES**

CHAPTER 8

MARSHALL ULRICH

"When people really get the book, they realize it's a love story. It's the highest compliment I receive." That's what Marshall Ulrich, my husband, says about his memoir, Running on Empty: An Ultramarathoner's Story of Love, Loss, and a Record-Setting Run Across America. Being the object of that love story is, well, a bit embarrassing—and the highest honor I have ever received. Marshall doesn't hold back anything in his book, including some pretty private details about himself, us, and our experiences. It's the way Marshall lives his life. He sets the bar highest for himself and always continues to set new goals, even now that he's in his 60s. But his résumé doesn't tell you who he is. His list of accomplishments is amazing, but it doesn't define who he is.

Marshall often says, "We all suffer from the human condition." We're all made of the same stuff. We have our strengths and our weaknesses. Things we're proud of and things we would do differently if we had the chance. We all feel pain and sorrow, as well as joy. We all have fears and doubts. Despite what some people may think, based solely on his accomplishments, Marshall is not superhuman, or an alien, or a king of endurance—or of anything else. Marshall is human, and he knows it. Perhaps this is his best quality, at least to me. He is funny and kind. Marshall loves his children more than anything, and he tells them that he's proud of them. He calls me his beautiful wife, even when I don't look or feel very beautiful. While some won't believe it, Marshall hurts, both physically and emotionally, just like the rest of us; he just does a better job at hiding it from most people, most of the time. He loves dogs—his dogs, any dogs. Maybe that's why his adventure racing team is the Stray Dogs. He's a loyal friend and has amazing, quality, long-time, wonderful, and loving friends—his family by choice, who he couldn't live without.

Marshall knows everyone can dig deeper and love more. Himself included. Me, too, of course. Marshall is good to me and good for me, and I can only strive to be the person he sees in me. I hope Marshall's "extreme" accomplishments—his story—will inspire you to find the amazing person you are, too.

–Heather Ulrich

DIG DEEPER AND LOVE MORE

By Scott Ludwig with Heather Ulrich

Dig deeper. That part Marshall Ulrich has down, at least if you consider feats of endurance. The love more part has been, on some levels, a greater challenge.

Raised on a dairy farm in Colorado, a hard day's work was the norm for Marshall. He learned a solid work ethic as well as how to take care of himself, whether in the dry heat of the summer with the sun beating down on the high plains or the frigid cold of the winter with the winds making the snow dance across the prairie. Young Marshall also dared to dream, fired by stories like *The Call of the Wild* and by watching mountain climbers, brought into his living room through the magic of black-and-white TV, struggle for survival as well as success.

"Someday, I want to do that," he proclaimed when he was only five. He had no reason to believe he couldn't do it. Failure is not an option for the wonders of youth, as everything seems possible and within reach—at least someday.

Maybe one of the most amazing things about Marshall is that he never let go of that wonder. He believes he—and, in fact, all of us—can do a lot more than we think we can. And he's set out to prove it over and over. Since strapping on low-top canvas Converse shoes for a 5K race in 1979, Marshall has continually pushed himself to the next level—from road marathons, to 100-mile trail ultramarathons, to multi-day, multi-sport, up-to-550-mile adventure races, to the highest and coldest peaks on earth. For decades his mantra was "as far as I can, as fast as I can." He also set out, every year, to do something no one else had done, things that some people thought might be impossible. But Marshall believed. He knew himself.

I need to be accepting of myself, know my limitations, and not talk myself out of anything.

One can only assume Marshall has never had much success with the latter.

Then you push forward anyway, step after step, even though every cell in your body tells you to stop. And you discover that you can go on.

–Marshall Ulrich, *Running on Empty*

In 1989, Marshall was the first person to complete every American 100-mile trail run in one calendar year (there were six at that time). In five out of six of those races, he finished in the top 10. In other words, he didn't hold back. He's won the Badwater Ultramarathon a record four times and still holds the record to the top of Mount Whitney—the original 146-mile course from the lowest to the highest point in the lower 48 states—almost a quarter of a century later. He directed and invited the toughest, strongest, and fastest athletes he knew to run 310 miles across Colorado, and then he beat them all—three times. He was the first person to complete the Death Valley Cup—the Badwater 135, a shortened version of the lowest-to-highest race across Death Valley, and the Furnace Creek 508, a 508-mile bicycle ride also across the Mojave Desert—in the same season.

Marshall was not only first, numerous times, but he also remains the *only* person to complete feats such as the Leadville Trail 100 and the Pikes Peak Marathon on the same weekend *(Is that even possible? Apparently it is!)* and the Leadville Triple Crown—a 100-mile bicycle race, a 100-mile run, and a 100-mile kayak—on consecutive weekends.

RUNNING TO EXTREMES

Obviously there are no limitations in this man's mind. But what about his heart? The farm boy from Colorado fell in love with his high school sweetheart. They married and had a little girl. Then he lost his beloved Jean to breast cancer when they were both only 30 years old. *Dig deeper.* Marshall has always continued to do this on a physical level, adding more and more to his résumé.

He's crossed Death Valley on foot in July and August a record 26 times, including a self-contained and unsupported solo crossing and a "quad" crossing covering 584 miles (from the Badwater basin to the summit of Mount Whitney, one side to the other and then repeat). In my book, *A Few Degrees from Hell,* I referred to Marshall as the "Desert Fox," a tribute to his prowess for running incredible distances in the desert. Taking it a step further, in 2013, he and his friend, Dave Heckman, completed the first-ever circumnavigation of Death Valley National Park—a 16-day, 425-mile, self-supported odyssey (they buried caches of water, food, and supplies outside of the park boundaries in advance of their trek) during the hottest month in U.S. history, a feat that may qualify him for the nickname "Desert Camel" as well.

In December 2001, *Outside* magazine tagged Marshall as an "Endurance King," a title he's more than earned by finishing more than 125 ultramarathons, averaging over 125 miles each. He dug deep outside of ultrarunning, too, when, mostly in his 40s, he completed 12 expedition-length adventure races, and he was one of only three people in the world to compete in all nine of the Eco Challenges, dubbed by creator Mark Burnett as "the world's premier adventure race." Then, in his 50s, he turned to the mountains, recalling those mountaineers he watched in black and white when he was only five years old, and climbed to the top of the highest mountain on every continent, including Mount Everest, all on first attempts.

So he was an Endurance King. So what? He still felt he had something to prove when, at the age of 57, Marshall became the third fastest person ever to run, walk, and occasionally hobble 3,063 miles in only 52.5 days from San Francisco to New York, setting a new Grand Masters (age 50 and over) record in the process. His adventures—the highs, the lows, and everything in between—are captured in his memoir, *Running on Empty: An Ultramarathoner's Story of Love, Loss, and a Record-Setting Run Across America* (Penguin, 2011). Here's one example of words his readers have found inspiring.

> "Keep going, one foot in front of the other, millions of times. Face forward and take the next step. Don't flinch when the road or going gets rough, you fall down, you miss a turn, or the bridge you planned to cross has collapsed. Do what you say you'll do, and don't let anything or anyone stop you. Deal with the obstacles as they come. Move on. Keep going, no matter what, one foot in front of the other, millions of times."
>
> –Marshall Ulrich, *Running on Empty*

Read what Dean Karnazes has to say about him:

Marshall is The Man. […] Nothing can stop him, and that gives us all hope, gives us resolve to keep trying.

Or this from Kara Goucher:

[...] a master of mental toughness, an endurance legend, and exactly the kind of example our country needs right now.

And one from Ray Zahab:

Strength tempered by calm, a glint of courage balanced with compassion and consideration, wisdom combined with experience.

Consider the sources of these comments. Dean, Kara, and Ray are three of the most prominent runners in the world, and there's a really good chance they know what they're talking about.

Yet a look at a Marshall's journal from his 2004 expedition to Mount Everest (at 29,035 feet, the highest point in the world) shows that he still has doubts.

"I am losing my strength, and there doesn't seem to be anything that I can do about it, except to go down.

I have an uneasy feeling about tomorrow, and what it might bring.

The anger comes from within me, and that anger is my inability to deal with my own inadequacies."

–Marshall Ulrich, private Mount Everest journal

Marshall has fears and feels pain just like the rest of us. Yet on Everest, and in so many other situations, he's able to *"keep going, no matter what, one foot in front of the other, millions of times."* Some of it comes from following a created and self-imposed set of rules that one of his friends titled "Marshall Law."

MARSHALL LAW

1. Expect a journey and a battle.

2. Focus on the present and set intermediate goals.

3. Don't dwell on the negative.

4. Transcend the physical.

5. Accept your fate.

6. Have confidence that you will succeed.

7. Know that there will be an end.

8. Suffering is okay.

9. Be kind to yourself.

10. Quitting is not an option.

–Marshall Ulrich, as developed for potential Navy Seal recruits and included in *Running on Empty*

RUNNING TO EXTREMES

But even Marshall Law doesn't explain it all. The farm boy with the broken heart accomplished a lot on a physical level but continued to struggle with loving more. He remarried, raised three kids, got divorced, ran a successful business, returned to his farming roots, continued to run, and lived and played high in the mountains. Still, he kept people—even his spouses and kids—at arm's length. He thought he could be an island unto himself, which hurt those closest to him more than he realized. It wasn't until he ran across America at the age of 57, with his wife Heather always at his side, holding him up, that he was able to find deep fulfillment in something greater than achievement. He realized that "being a runner doesn't make you a sage....it doesn't make you a good person, or even a nice person." Marshall Ulrich would never "presume to tell you who to be or how to live," but he does know this:

"...everyone can dig deeper and love more."

–Marshall Ulrich, *Running on Empty*

Postscript: In July 2015, Marshall Ulrich completed his 20th Badwater 146 race. Staying true to the original idea of the race, he always travels on foot in July from the Badwater basin at 282 feet below sea level, the lowest point in North America, to the 14,505-foot summit of Mount Whitney, the highest point in the lower 48 states. He is also working on his second book, **Both Feet on the Ground,** *which will spotlight his athletic pursuits and exploration, including adventure racing and mountaineering and the importance of connecting to the natural world.*

MARSHALL ULRICH

RUNNING TO **EXTREMES**

CHAPTER 9

PAM REED

Most people are aware that Pam Reed won the Badwater Ultramarathon in 2002 and 2003. In 2002, she finished over four hours in front of the second-place competitor and male champion. In 2003, she reached the finish line at the portals of Mount Whitney over 24 minutes ahead of the second-place competitor and male champion. In 2003, that man was none other than Dean Karnazes.

In 2003, I competed in Badwater, as well, but ultimately the 130-plus temperatures didn't play nice with my body, and I was forced to drop out.

In 2006, I offered my services as a crewmember for Pam. I had a falling out with the race director but really wanted to be in on the induction of Jack Denness and Rhonda Provost into the Badwater Hall of Fame, so crewing for Pam was my way of "worming" my way back into the Badwater family. As it turned out, Pam had medical issues that year and was forced to drop out. I was really hoping to help Pam set another record, but knowing she wanted me to pace her up the Panamint grade later in the race probably would have doomed her for sure anyway.

Pam is a hard person to get to know as she is usually very quiet and one of the most humble people I've ever met. She just likes to run and set records.

–Ben Jones

RUNNING TO EXTREMES

RUNNING IS MY SANITY

By Bonnie Busch

A slender, tanned woman made her way over to the patio furniture where I sat, enjoying the shade. Carefully juggling a morning beverage and a cell phone, she approached and politely asked if she could join me. I nodded in approval and made a nonchalant offer to remove my feet from a chair I was using to rest my weary legs. She waved off the need for me to move and made herself comfortable in another chair at the table. Despite not having slept for the last two days, I couldn't sleep, and I couldn't think. Someone had moved this pool furniture onto the lawn in the shade and facing the street. From here, we could see the traffic, cars, and people who might be running or walking on their way to finish the race. The morning temperature was already warm and getting warmer fast. We exchanged a few polite sentences about our own race before we opened up about how we really did. We talked about the journey, and I thought we would eventually get around to the results. Periodically she would check her watch so that she could phone her mother early, but not *too* early. She was concerned about a photograph that may have made the paper, and she felt it needed an explanation. Time passed quickly. Members of our respective crews eventually found us on the lawn and reminded us of other tasks that demanded our attention. We parted as easily as we started, and she finally made her phone call. The year was 2003, and I would later learn that I was talking to the woman who had just won the 135-mile Badwater Ultramarathon. First place not only among the women, but the men as well. For the second year in a row, as a matter of fact. Funny—she failed to mention that.

Pam's rookie Badwater year had come just 12 months earlier in 2002 when a friend convinced her that this was the perfect race for her—lots and lots of miles, and lots and lots of heat. That friend, Chuck Giles, had witnessed the race and was convinced that an active crew could make a big difference with the right runner. Pam prepared to run, and her friends, Chuck and Susy Bacal, prepared a team to crew. Pam ran. Pam ran in the heat and hills around Tucson, Arizona. She put in hours in a sauna to get comfortable with the heat. She thought about the 135 miles; it would be longer than any race she had run before. She thought about the pavement, the sun, the heat, and the help of a ready crew. Using a variety of shorter races, Pam got ready for Badwater. She felt confident yet somewhat unsure of the outcome. There was only one way to find out.

The Badwater Ultramarathon 135 is an ultramarathon through Death Valley, California, during the hottest part of the summer. The area has the distinction of being, on average, the hottest place on the planet. The genesis for the race came when Al Arnold recognized the lowest point in the northern hemisphere was 146 miles away from the highest point Mount Whitney in the contiguous 48 states that make up the United States. In 1977, Al traversed the distance on foot. The start was at 282 feet below sea level at a landmark in Death Valley named Badwater, and his run finished on the summit of Mount Whitney at an elevation of 14,494 feet. As the word spread of Arnold's accomplishment, others would attempt the run under similar circumstances in the middle of summer so that they, too, could realize the full effects of the climate. Eventually, it became an organized race.

Today the race is 135 miles long and run completely on paved asphalt roads. Safety and environmental concerns caused a compromise years ago that cut off the last 11 miles of the race that had been conducted on the trail leading to the summit of Mount Whitney. Many race participants still choose to honor the original course that inspired the race by continuing to the summit with appropriate permits, gear, and supplies. Most wait until the day after they finish the race.

Pam's preparations were on target, and her race efforts had good results. Pam gives her crew much credit for adapting to conditions and being attentive to her needs as well as each other. At 41, Pam won the 2002 Badwater Ultramarathon with a new women's course record of 27 hours, 56 minutes, and 47 seconds. She was the only finisher under 30 hours and, perhaps most exciting, first overall. Her closest competitor was over four-and-a-half hours back, emerging from a strong men's field. Yes, things worked out rather well. The outcome got a fair amount of attention in the ultrarunning community and generated much interest beyond its cult-like followers. As the general media would report the human-interest story, some would begin to speculate. Pam had a lucky rookie race, a solidly attentive crew made the running easy, an easy 6:00 a.m. start in the cooler temperatures gave Pam a head start, and with rookie status Pam was able to run under the radar, going unnoticed from a competitive challenge and such.

While people were talking, Pam was out running. Less than a month after that rookie Badwater finish, Pam would toe the line at Leadville Trail 100 Run, a high altitude run in Colorado. Less than a month after that she would find her way to the Wasatch Front 100-Mile Endurance Run, another mountain run. Seventh woman in 24:45:32 at Leadville and second woman in 28:37:15 at Wasatch. Somewhere in that magical year, Pam also broke three hours at a marathon. Her confidence went up a notch. With ultrarunning reports generally focusing on single race results instead of the overall sport and correlating results, Pam could remain nearly anonymous.

Of course, Pam applied for the 2003 Badwater Ultramarathon. Why? Perhaps to prove she earned her 2002 finish; perhaps to prove she was not a one-hit wonder; perhaps because she had found a race that was perfect for her like her crew chief had suggested; or perhaps just to run a race she liked. She trained and raced hard with lots of miles. It seems that Pam much prefers racing to training. In a bold move just a month before her second Badwater race, Pam finished the 100-mile Western States Endurance Run in 23:47:01. Certainly a test of fitness but hardly specific to the demands of the road through Death Valley.

The 2003 Badwater Ultramarathon had assigned Pam a 10:00 a.m. starting time (a time reserved for the strongest competitors; the other start times are at 6 and 8 a.m.) along with the strongest competitors on paper. Pam started her day very similarly to 2002, trying to focus on her own race instead of the many distractions. But it was a very different race. The first checkpoint at approximately mile 17 found Pam just two minutes ahead of her time the prior year and running in fourth place overall. By the second checkpoint at roughly 42 miles, Pam was 10 minutes slower than the year before. The competition and the day were heating up. The early temperatures were about 10 degrees warmer than usual, and it would just get worse with the wind acting as a multiplier. Everyone expected heat, but this was more than what anyone had imagined. Pam's crew would adopt a replenish cycle with Pam that was as short as a half- or quarter-mile, while making any interaction brief and efficient. Everyone would suffer. Ice was quickly depleted, supplies tapped out, times at the mandatory checkpoints grew, many crew members were becoming ill, the medical staff was taxed, and the list of withdrawals was growing. Crew vehicles were reporting temperatures well in excess of 130 degrees Fahrenheit.

As the sun dipped low on the horizon, the wind was howling, beating anything in its path with heat. The lack of sun gave only a small degree of relief to the Badwater caravan crawling across the desert. Pam found herself a consistent 40 minutes behind the leaders and 42 minutes later than her 2002 time at the third checkpoint roughly halfway into the race. In the next 15 miles of climb, Pam would pass one of two leaders. Time to dig and continue to push to get this over with.

As day two came into full bloom, the efforts of the day and night before wore on everyone. The leader would hit a fast decline and would relinquish first place to Pam with about 100 miles under their feet. Pam could not relax. Runners behind her continued to push as she and they had done for hours and hours and hours, and they weren't done yet.

RUNNING TO EXTREMES

The long-time race leader would drop another spot, and the third-place competitor moved up to second. The updates coming to Pam were nerve wracking; she couldn't relax with the lead. Pam honored the lead with her continued effort marching up the significant grade those last 13 miles. Pam would finish in 28:26:52, first place over all. Again. The next competitor, Dean Karnazes, would finish some 25 minutes later. The two of them would be the only 2003 finishers to complete the race in less than 30 hours. Pam would never enjoy running anonymity again.

The media attention to the 2003 race spilled the news out of every pore. Ultramarathon news was hitting the mainstream. The uncharacteristic attention caused interest and plenty of debate in and out of the ultrarunning community. Should the sport stay out of the limelight or push into the mainstream? Should ultrarunners be paid to perform? Should ultrarunners be considered athletes like other sports or gifted oddities? Were women better endurance athletes? Should anybody be running that far? Could ultrarunners motivate the masses or simply cultivate a freak show mentality? Should races be able to traverse government parks, preserves, protected environments, or fragile ecosystems, putting hundreds of people on single-track trails in distant remote locations without adequate restrooms, easy emergency access, or minimum communication capabilities? People in the spotlight almost became assigned to one position or another based on a couple of unrelated quotes, and the dialog would live on. Pam was in the news, and, whether she realized it or not, she couldn't avoid the fray.

Pam kept running. Less than a month after that second Badwater win, Pam finished the Leadville Trail 100 Run, fifth woman in 27:14:46. Elsewhere in the ultrarunning community, people were trying to put together a U.S. national team to compete at the world 24-hour championships in less than two months. Pam's name was on their minds, but they didn't see specific race experience at a timed event. Could Pam cope with the repetition? These were people who evidently had not seen the long expanses of road that a Badwater runner faces. A destination in sight requiring almost a half a day of running to get there. Yes, she could cope with unchanging scenery. Pam was invited to join the U.S. team for the trip to the Netherlands. She honored her assignment with a 134.86-mile effort, sixth woman, becoming the first U.S. woman finisher and helping the U.S. women's team to a fourth-place finish.

But Pam's amazing year wasn't over. About a month after her assignment with the U.S. 24-hour team, Pam would step on to a track in California for the U.S. 24-hour championships. A packed, talented field began to circle the track, and, as we all know, it isn't who is ahead at 6 hours or even 12, but who is ahead at the very end that matters. Pam recorded steady miles, one mile after another, one hour after another. In the end, Pam had accumulated 138.959 miles, winning the women's race with a new U.S. women's 24-hour track record, snagging a 200,000-meter record for her age group along the way and placing fourth overall. If you were keeping track, that's five major and distinctly different races with great outcomes in about a six-month period in 2003 for Pam.

Success was years, maybe decades, in the making. Growing up in upper Michigan in a small town and attending a small school, Pam got consumed in gymnastics, then cheerleading, then tennis, and then eventually track. Fueled by competition and willing to put in the hard work to achieve results, Pam would focus and excel, often confused by others her age that were in sports for other benefits. As she moved from high school to college and into marriages and then children of her own, Pam remained active—playing tennis, practicing yoga, and teaching aerobics—and always running, a little more all the time. Pam trains three to five hours each day, ever since about the seventh grade, with very few exceptions. She figured out how to squeeze in her running in small doses between errands and obligations, a skill perfected when the kids were at home. She politely points out that she enjoys running and racing, while maintaining a dislike for training. She subscribes to a common fitness model of ultrarunners: maintaining a level of fitness that allows her to run a decent marathon at any time.

To suggest Pam has not had injuries or disappointments in her running would be untrue. She remembers many of them with specific detail. When recounting them, she includes a lesson-learned summary. Not overthinking the cause and effects, Pam puts these into broader perspective, adapts, and then moves on. Each served a purpose, building blocks to a life of running. Like many runners, Pam has gone through cycles of being injury free as well as periods of time when she was riddled with injuries. She isn't shy about seeking new or old traditional methods of treatment, as long as they deliver results.

Pam now calls Wyoming home with a "regular" job: race director. Pam owns and operates the Tucson Marathon in Arizona, having started it in 1995. The race offers a marathon, half marathon, and relay. Pam is also owner and co-director of the Jackson Hole Half Marathon in Wyoming. Her children have moved on to secondary education and jobs, so downsizing is a current activity. Pam is still running, putting in memorable races at a rate that is rare in ultrarunning. She still experiments with a variety of terrain and race formats. It's common to see Pam put in a couple of big races a month. To date, her record collection includes these U.S. women's records recognized by USA Track & Field:

- 100 miles, track, age group 40-44:   16:48:31
- 200,000 meters, track, age group 40-44: 21:14:16
- 24 hours, track: 223,633 meters (138.595 miles)
- 48 hours, track: 354,669 meters (220.381 miles)
- Six day, road: 490 miles

And, yes, throw in a 300-mile continuous run *(no sleep!)* in less than 80 hours. She has completed 10 or more finishes at Badwater and Wasatch and is quickly closing in on 10 at some of the most widely sought out and challenging ultramarathon races in the country: Western States Endurance Run and Leadville Trail 100 Run. Throw in some triathlons at Ironman distance (2.4-mile swim, 112-mile bike, and 26.2-mile run), having finished 44 Ironman races, which includes five trips to their World Championships in Hawaii. Pam is finishing about four to six Ironman races a year since getting back into them in 2006. Pam Reed is not one to sit still.

Because she doesn't.

What running will Pam be doing 5, 10, or 20 years from now? Pam won't predict because her primary focus is on doing what she is doing now. Her appetite for running, racing, and doing all the work that goes into it is driven by enjoyment and doing as much as she can as long as she is enjoying it. She does not take running for granted; she enjoys each run and very much appreciates the fact that she is still able to lace up her shoes every day to do just that. A good bet for the future would be that she follows the advice she has often given to others: Be active, find something you like to do, and do it.

As you may have gathered, Pam loves to run.

Postscript: Pam says she feels blessed to still be running and never takes it for granted. She tries her best to protect it and enjoy it—something that's not always easy when she's in the middle of a 100-mile run. It continues to amaze her that people can actually run 100 miles or more.

RUNNING TO **EXTREMES**

CHAPTER 11

LARRY MACON

If you cannot hear him at a marathon before you see him, that's because he's not there. If he were there, you would know it.

If you're looking for an athletic, fast runner, you are looking for the wrong person. He lacks a head full of hair or a graceful stride, and he is an attorney, but try not to hold that against him.

If you want to meet someone who is possessed instead of obsessed, you have found the right person. He has to wear different size shoes on each foot to be able to run and wears more layers than an onion, seldom shedding any of them.

Most weekends he schedules several marathons and chooses the ones with the tightest flight connections to make it more interesting. Every year he completes the 50 states, inspires thousands of runners, makes the sport more colorful with his boisterous laughter, and completes more marathons than most runners do in a lifetime.

Once you meet him, you will never forget him.

–Steve Boone

RUNNING TO **EXTREMES**

THE QUINTESSENTIAL MARATHON MAN

By Marsha White

I first met Guinness World Record holder Larry Macon back in 2009 when I was a novice marathoner. Over the years, other runners kept pointing him out to me, saying he is famous for running the most marathons of any man in a year (105 in 2008, 106 in 2010, 113 in 2011, 157 in 2012, and 255 in 2013). I was in awe and way too shy to introduce myself, especially since he always seemed to be surrounded by hordes of admirers. There were times when we ran by each other during races, but all I could muster was a wave and a smile. Larry would respond with a huge laugh and a loud "howdy."

Flash forward to 2011. I was emboldened by my record of over 100 marathons and ultras accomplished over the past four years. I was now a 50 States Marathon Club finisher and an eight-star member of Marathon Maniacs. Though my times were not fast, and I was never competitive, I had gained confidence and experience from doing so many races and meeting so many like-minded racers. Now, when I would run into Larry at races, we would exchange greetings and chat about our latest exploits; often these talks would involve commiserating about the weather. Both of us dislike extremely cold temperatures, so we could easily identify each other at races because we were the runners covered in multiple layers of clothing, balaclavas on our faces, and mittens on our hands while everyone else was dressed in shorts and singlets.

When I learned of the opportunity to interview Larry firsthand for this story, I was excited. Now I would finally have a chance to uncover the secrets that motivate the "iron man" of marathoning and learn what keeps him moving. Maybe I could adopt some of those secrets and put them to use in my own attempts at tallying up distance races. It turned out that the most difficult part of meeting with Larry was finding a time when he was not traveling or running. Originally I had hoped to interview him while we were both doing the same race. That would be a unique idea, I thought, and even though I might miss some valuable insights while trying to maintain a reasonable pace and reach the finish line, it was not an impossible task. There are times when my fastest mile approaches Larry's slowest, and we can move in concert with each other. However, our schedules never did mesh sufficiently, and though we saw each other unexpectedly at some races, there was never a time to plan for a real interview.

Even catching Larry by phone was a major accomplishment given our diverse schedules and time zone challenges. We finally managed to "meet" by phone in October of 2014. At that time, Larry was working toward completing 150 marathons for the current year. In 2013, he had achieved 255 marathon finishes, bringing his total to well over 1,000. He has completed the 50-states circuit more than 16 times, with eight of those in one calendar year. The numbers are astounding, especially considering that he began his marathoning career in 1996 at 52 years of age. In his "other" life, Larry is a board-certified trial lawyer in San Antonio, Texas, with over 30 years of legal expertise.

Rather than paraphrase our telephone conversation, I thought the best way to maintain the integrity of our interview would be to keep the question-and-answer format, with some slight editing and an occasional parenthetical comment. What follows is the result of our conversation. (Please imagine that Larry's words are spoken with a pleasant Texas drawl, and, yes, you may add a slight Boston twang to my questions.)

RUNNING TO **EXTREMES**

MW: When did you get started in marathoning?

LM: Some lawyer friends and I would get together for coffee after work and tell tall tales about what we had been doing over the weekend. Some would brag that they played three rounds of golf or swam two miles, but all were exaggerating at least a little bit. When they asked me what I had done, I did not want to admit that I had worked hard all week and had not done one lick of exercise. I glanced at a newspaper, saw the word "marathon," and told everyone I was training for a marathon. "Wonderful," was the reply, "the San Antonio marathon is coming up in three weeks." I realized I was stuck; now I had to spend the next three weeks getting in shape for the race. The moral of the story is, don't lie!

MW: So, the [old] San Antonio marathon in 1996 was your first marathon attempt. How did you do?

LM: [laughing] Not that much worse than I do in races now. It was about 110 degrees in the shade, and I stumbled along, half walked, half ran, and, thank God, somehow crossed the finish line. Most people would have said 'that's it,' but not me. I enjoyed it even though I couldn't walk for three days afterward. I liked talking with people and being outdoors. However poor my form was and regardless of how I felt during the race, I had a real feeling of accomplishment when it was all over.

MW: Were you athletic in high school and college?

LM: I grew up in Texas, and everybody in Texas played football. I tried, but I was terrible. I couldn't do anything else, so they put me on the offensive line so I could stand in people's way. I weighed 170 pounds, and the other tackle weighed 240, but I was listed as 200 pounds in the schedule just so the other players wouldn't immediately run all over me. I spent most of the games with cleat marks all over my face.

MW: What criteria do you use in deciding what races to do?

LM: My criteria have changed over the years. At first I was trying to finish the states several times, usually within a year. Aside from that, I try to run at least two marathons a weekend, and [some typical Larry humor here] I try to get them as far apart as possible to make travel more difficult. My rule was that I couldn't count them as a double unless they were in two different time zones. If races are too close together, then they are for sissies.

About a year ago, I drove 16 hours to get from one race to another; it should have taken just 12 hours, but it was pouring rain and the streets were flooding. I got within five miles of the second race, but I couldn't see clearly. I made a turn, and all of a sudden I saw a wave of water rushing toward me. The wave lifted my car and flung it into a ditch, and then the car filled up with water. Somehow I managed to climb out of the car. There was no house for miles around and no cell phone signal, so I began to walk. All of a sudden, a sheriff came out of nowhere and started to write me three tickets. I asked the sheriff to drive me someplace so I could get a ride, but the sheriff replied, "Nope, that's not my job." Then he said I was a very lucky man. Puzzled, I looked at him and explained that I had spent lots of money to get to a race which I now will miss; I will have to pay lots more money to Hertz to get the rental car fixed; I've been out in the rain for hours; and I'm cold and soaked and now I have to walk a couple of miles for help. I asked the sheriff, "Please, sir, explain to me why am I so lucky?" "Well," he replied, "one of the tickets I gave you was for not obeying a traffic sign. That sign said 'Warning, Bridge Out.' If that wave had not knocked your car off the road, you would be dead now!" That was quite an experience. But the bottom line is that I try to make my races as challenging as possible, so I can make a fool of myself or make sure I can be dead last.

RUNNING TO EXTREMES

MW: Do you ever repeat certain races?

LM: Yes, many times. There are lots of really fun races I do over and over again. There is a race in Juneau, Alaska, that I have done over 10 times and a double in New Hampshire and Maine every fall that I have done a number of times. Those are not that far apart, so I am a little ashamed of that.

MW: Who makes your travel plans? Do you have a secretary or administrative assistant to help make reservations, register for races, and make travel arrangements? [I find this to be a daunting assignment myself, so I figured Larry must have help, especially since his plans are so much more complex than mine.]

LM: I make all my own travel plans. It is far too complicated to explain everything to my secretary. It is not that difficult, just a matter of plugging on through and doing it. But I admit that it is sometimes harder than running the marathon. I keep track of my races on an Excel spreadsheet, but I do occasionally make mistakes. Sometimes I register for a race twice, or I will show up for a race but forget to register beforehand. On the last day of the Tahoe Triple, I had someone who was supposed to pick up my race packet for me but the race director [RD] could not find me registered. The RD did let me register late for that one, even though registration was officially closed.

I often have a second backup race planned just in case something happens, and I can't make it to my first choice. Sometimes I have to call the RD at home and beg him or her to let me in. I'd say I have about a 90 percent record of success in getting into my second race.

MW: What about injuries? It's unusual to run so many races so close together without any ill consequences.

LM: I've been extremely lucky. The only problem I experienced occurred two summers ago. For some reason, my friend, Jim Simpson [another 1,000+ marathoner], and I got what I call "old man's lean disease," when you start leaning to one side and your ears bang into your ankles. It was weird because we got this malady at the same time. He was leaning to the left, and I was leaning to the right, so we looked like the letter H. I went to two different orthopedists. They started me on two different rehabilitation programs, and I did them both. That's the only thing I've ever had go wrong.

MW: What do you do, if anything, to prevent injuries?

LM: Prevention? I'm not sure. Maybe it's because I've been a vegetarian for more than 30 years, but it may also be just blind luck. God protects drunks and fools, and I am both.

MW: Is there anything you do post-race to hasten recovery?

LM: [Laughing] I jump in a car and drive as fast as I can to the nearest airport, preferably with wet clothes on, ready for my next adventure. Seriously, though, I always have chocolate milk. It's just wonderful. A lot of things you liked as a kid are really good for you as an adult as well.

MW: How do you deal with fatigue from doing so many races so close together?

LM: I don't get really tired. I did a lot of races in the last two years, but as long as I had a little bit of sleep afterward I was fine. During the week, I get four hours a night. The night before a marathon, I like to get five to six hours, but sometimes I end up with only three or four. They say sleep helps your brain, but obviously it hasn't helped me at all. No problems with jet lag either. I fly over 300,000 miles a year, at least a third for work.

MW: Speaking of work, how do you manage to fit in racing while also working full-time as an attorney?

LM: [Laughing] Work? I'm a lawyer, and being a lawyer doesn't require work; it's about the easiest job around. [More laughter] Seriously though, I work long hours in my office until eight or nine every night that I am home. Nowadays, with computers and the Internet, it is easy to get work done on the road. On several occasions, I have even worked while doing a race. I took an hour-long conference call once while I was running Boston. And during some of the Mainly Marathon races [a no-time limit series], I will stop and take a call. [I can attest firsthand to watching Larry "at work" during some races.]

MW: What occupies your time when you are not working or running?

LM: I have a fulfilling home life. I am married, and we have five dogs, a cat, and a wallaby at our house. My wife, Jane, has a ranch with mini-longhorns, miniature horses, and llamas. My goal in life is to *not* help out with her ranch. But I have plenty to keep me busy.

MW: What about favorite brand of running shoes?

LM: I really have no choice when it comes to shoes. I wear New Balance 1540, not only because I love them but also because they come in 6E width. I have an enormous bunion on my left foot, and this is the only shoe that comes in that size [11 6E]. Two medical people have told me that I should have surgery on that bunion, but they cautioned that surgery would mean I would probably never be able to run again. If I keep on running as I am now, I will continue to have pain, but as long as I can stand it, I will. It seems I have a high tolerance for such pain, so I am going to keep running—it can't get much worse. It does hurt when I put on my running shoes, and it hurts terribly when I'm done.

MW: Do you prefer road or trail races? Flat or rolling? Cold temperatures or warm?

LM: If I want to stay upright, I prefer road. I don't consider it a real trail race unless I've done a couple of face-plants. There was a trail race in North Carolina called the Triple Lakes, and they posted pictures of my knee one year after I fell about 20 times during the race. I've never broken anything. I swear every year I will never run another trail race, and then my schedule calls for one. Roots and rocks are hazardous for me, especially toward the end of the race when I am not picking up my feet.

I like flat, though there are beautiful downhill races in Utah. I definitely prefer warm temperatures. When it's cold, I have a particular costume I wear: tights, gloves, and balaclava. If it gets below 80, I am cold. I did a race in California, and it was 65, and I wouldn't take off my gloves. I'm too fragile and delicate.

MW: What about training? And days off for rest and recovery?

LM: I don't train with all the racing I do on weekends. On my days away from running, I do some stretching, weightlifting, and yoga. Any day I am not racing is a rest day for me—and even when I am racing, I sometimes consider that a rest day, too. [I am pretty sure Larry is kidding when he says that.]

MW: Have you done any international races?

LM: I thought the Quebec City Marathon was gorgeous. I used to run half marathons in Mexico, since it is so close to San Antonio, but it has become too dangerous lately. I love to travel and have been to Africa five times as well as to India and Vietnam. I made a deal with my wife, though, that I wouldn't run any marathons when we travel together. Two years ago we were in India, and I was sorely tempted to do a race that was supposed to be held the next day, but I resisted. Jane does travel with me to races on occasion, especially those that are in exciting places. She comes with me to the doubles in Hawaii in January and Anchorage in July, as well as a quad in Seattle over Thanksgiving. She stays home when I travel to Iowa and Indiana.

MW: How about ultramarathons? I know I've seen you at FANS and a few other timed races.

LM: I frequently do 50Ks, but they are not much different than a marathon. I've done one 50-miler just so I can say I have done one. I also have done a lot of 12-hour races, but I only do enough mileage to meet Marathon Maniac criteria. [In timed races over eight hours, participants must complete at least the 50K distance.] I have no desire to go any longer than that.

MW: What has been your favorite race to date?

LM: My favorite race is always the one I am doing at the moment. It doesn't matter what the weather or circumstances may be; I always enjoy the current race and think it is the best.

MW: Any races you didn't like; ones you would never do again?

LM: There are some that are very difficult or that are very hot, cold, snowy, or rainy. For me, cold is much worse than heat. In Minot, North Dakota, I was signed up for a race at the end of April. I thought by that time it would be nice and warm, but instead the weather was terrible: wind chill below zero with snow and sleet. Two hundred people had registered for the race, but only 50 showed up, and, of course, I was one of them. The race director finally called the race when I was at mile 18; nobody finished.

I have another snow story, also in April, but this time in Wisconsin. I once again expected warmer temperatures, so all I had on was shorts and a singlet. I went around to people in the crowd begging for some warmer clothes. One guy gave me a jacket, and a girl handed me some tights. I didn't realize until later that the tights had "run like a girl" printed all over them; I was just thankful to have them on my legs. During that same race, I was slipping and sliding on the snow. A woman saw me sliding all over the place and mentioned that I should ask at the next aid station for some screws to put on my shoes; the volunteers were using a battery-powered screwdriver to install the screws. She had them on her feet, and she boasted how well she was managing to deal with the snow. As she said this, her feet hit a rock, and she slid horizontally, ending up with a broken leg. I decided to forego the screws and continued on my merry, if slippery way.

At another race, I was shaking so badly from the cold and rain at the end of a race I couldn't get into my car without help. And once I was inside, I couldn't turn the ignition to start the car. Both times I had to ask someone to open the door and then start my car so I could get the heater going.

There are some races where the race directors try intentionally to make the courses difficult and almost impossible to finish. One year I ran a race in New Jersey called the Muddy Marathon; there were 28 starters and only 7 finishers. I won the master's division because there was no one over the age of 40 dumb enough to run the race except me. The race director was disappointed that so many runners finished and planned to make it harder the following year.

RUNNING TO EXTREMES

Another such race is the NipMuck Marathon in Connecticut. I signed up and headed in my rental car to the race site, carrying my GPS system, my map of the course, and some Gatorade. The bottle of Gatorade leaked and shorted out my GPS and completely dissolved the paper map, so I ended up arriving an hour late to the race start. I asked the race director if I could still run. He replied, "Yes, I would love to see you fail." With a challenge like that, I ran like crazy and somehow finished.

MW: What was your most memorable race?

LM: That would have to be Boston in 2013, the year of the bombings. I felt like I was doing well that day. I heard a couple of ambulance sirens in the distance, but spectators seemed unconcerned at that point. By the time I arrived at mile 25, there were 12 policeman with automatic weapons lined up across the street, just before the famous Citgo sign. They said, "STOP! The race is over." I explained that I needed to go to the finish to get my stuff and get back to my hotel but to no avail. They told all of us that we would have to stay right where we were, and in two or three hours buses would come to pick us up.

By this time, dozens of runners were crowding around, and many were in tears. After all, Boston is the gold standard for marathoners, and many people only get to do the race once. I decided I was not going to simply stand around and wait. I began to knock on doors at various homes and establishments along the street. Cell phones were not usable. A person in a local synagogue opened the door and told me about the bombing and what was happening at the finish line. He was gracious enough to let me use his landline phone to contact my hotel (which said the police wouldn't let me in to get my belongings even if I could get there) and my airline (American Airlines said there was only one plane, and it was ready to leave). I could not get a taxi or a car rental service to pick me up because no cars were allowed in or out of the perimeter zone.

But I knew I only had about 1.2 miles to go to get to the finish line. I asked a car rental service if they could pick me up if I could manage to meet them at a point just beyond the zone. The answer was yes, so I started to run. The police, of course, wanted to know where I was going, but I simply responded that I was just out for a run. What's another mile or two under the circumstances? I met up with the car service, managed to get to the airport, get through TSA with just my driver's license, and then discovered my flight had been delayed. I always carry my license with me on races, but I had no credit cards or cash or checks, and I was desperate at that point for something to eat. I chose a restaurant, explained my situation, and when the server learned I had just run Boston, he gave me the meal on the house.

Once I made it on the plane, everyone turned to stare at me; here I was, perspiring, dressed in singlet and shorts, with no baggage or anything else. The flight attendant explained my situation, and then I had to fend off all the drinks that people began sending my way. But the story doesn't end there. After I arrived in San Antonio, I had no cash or keys to get to my home or back in my house. Fortunately, people are wonderful, and the taxi driver took me home gratis. A week later, the hotel sent my clothes and keys back to me. I did Boston again this year for the 11th time [Larry runs Boston for the American Liver Foundation], and while there were lots of police and people were tense, the experience was very uplifting.

MW: What advice do you have for runners who want to do lots of marathons?

LM: I have two suggestions: First, get rid of your watch—don't worry about your finishing time. I have been dead last in races in almost every state, and I have also won my age group in many races. Finishing times are not as important as enjoying each race. Second, talk to people—it is possible to make wonderful friends at these races.

RUNNING TO EXTREMES

MW: Any future goals?

LM: To keep running until I drop!

Postscript: Larry Macon now has run more than 1,450 marathons and ultras.

He has now established Guinness World Records for the most marathons in a year five times, the most recent being 2013 with 239.

He has run a marathon in all 50 states 19 times, including all 50 in a calendar year nine times.

Larry was Maniac of the Year seven times and was selected for the Marathon Maniac Hall of Fame.

Finally, Larry has won exactly one race: The Bear Lake Marathon in Idaho in 2008. Just don't ask him how many participants there were.

LARRY MACON

RUNNING TO EXTREMES

CHAPTER 12

TIM TWIETMEYER

En route to the Western States Endurance Run weekend kick-off at Squaw Valley, Tim and I decided to stop at a Starbucks for a cup of joe and a snack. We went through the drive-thru, and the barista was very friendly. She looked at Tim and said he looked familiar. "Are you guys runners?" Then she looked across to the front passenger seat, and she said, "Oh my god, oh my god, oh my god!" (Definitely a Harry Met Sally coffee shop moment) "My dad has a poster of you in his house. Are you Tim Twietmeyer?" I instantly started to crack up. The expression on Tim's face while he was slamming down a piece of coffee cake chipmunk-style was pure boyish innocence. He said, "Yes." That was it. The "oh my gods" ensued, I continued to crack up, and Tim was just totally speechless. He had that girl in the palm of his hand—just like a rock star! We said goodbye and drove away. In the rearview mirror, I can still see the image of her head hanging out of the drive-thru window like a giraffe. We cracked up about it the whole way to the Western States Endurance Run, and we talk about it every year at our annual trail work campout. He is, indeed, a humble guy...

–Mark Falcone

RUNNING TO EXTREMES

AVERAGE JOE

By Bonnie Busch

Married with three children. College graduate with a professional career. Been with the same employer for more than 30 years. Volunteers in the community. A few inches over six feet and maybe one hundred sixty- or seventy-something pounds. Tries to eat right and stay active. Is Tim Twietmeyer another average Joe?

He might be just another face in a crowd of runners, but he is certainly not anonymous when standing around a pre-dawn start line for a 100-mile trail run that begins in Squaw Valley, California. Known as the Western States Endurance Run, it was the genesis for 100-mile trail races in the United States. The race was, and still is, one of the most sought-after races for an ultrarunner's résumé. As a runner, Tim left an indelible mark on the race with 5 wins, 15 top-five finishes, a 17:17 master's division course record (until 2010), and a tidy collection of 25—actually all of his finishes—under 24 hour.

So how does an average Joe get started in ultrarunning? While in junior college, Tim happened upon a flyer describing a 24-hour running event nearby. Curiosity drove him to check it out. "Fascinating" is the word he uses to describe what he saw. Participants never seemed to stop moving; they weren't real fast, but they were certainly persistent. Eating and drinking while maintaining some semblance of forward motion. Running with periodic walking breaks were repeated. The miles added up. Don Choi would break an American record, and others, including Dick Collins and Ruth Anderson, would also lay down some impressive totals on the cinder track. That day in 1978 is an easy recall for Tim and still gets him excited.

In 1979, Tim joined the ultramarathon ranks with his first race of a distance longer than a marathon: a 50-mile finish. College and life demands pushed racing a little further down on the priority list. Eventually Tim got around to finishing 100 miles on a track for a race qualifier and then tackled his first Western States run in 1981. Twenty-two-year-old Tim would complete the race in 22:03, 25th overall. It was a solid start to an ultrarunning career that would parallel the evolution of the sport. In fact, it wouldn't be an exaggeration to suggest he may have been one of the driving forces behind it.

Think back to 1981: Jimmy Carter turned the job of United States President over to Ronald Reagan, who would months later take a bullet in the chest, nominate the first woman to the U.S. Supreme Court, and fire striking air traffic controllers who refused to return to work. The country was in a recession. Muhammad Ali would lose his last professional boxing match, and Walter Cronkite did the nightly news for the last time. Johnny Carson hosted the Academy Awards, and *Ordinary People* won best picture and best director. The Centers for Disease Control and Prevention would report on a rare form of pneumonia found only in people with weakened immune systems; this would be the first reported case of AIDS. The Rolling Stones started their Tattoo You tour, and the band Metallica was formed.

One could find shoes to run in at sporting goods stores, although seldom shoes specifically designed for running. Running stores per se were a rare commodity. Packs to run with were homemade or simply pockets sewn into clothing; hydration bottles were whatever one could find; and technical clothes were nothing more than a far-off dream. Homemade potions were the equivalent of today's gels, blocks, and tablets. Aid station food was either bring your own or a simple selection of peanut butter and jelly sandwiches, soup crackers, and hard candy. Knowledge and news of ultrarunning relied on periodic magazines, very rare news stories, chance encounters for word-of-mouth exchanges, and one's own discovery and experiences. Tools of the trade evolved slowly.

Tim trained like many of the few ultrarunners around at the time, using marathons as training runs. Chaining a few of those together seemed like it would prepare one for running longer distances. Races were small, often simple affairs, but do enough of these in a small geographic area, and you begin to see the same faces either as a participant, volunteer, or crew. Conversation and exchange of information ensued. A few individuals were writing about their endurance experiences, so an eager runner could devour their text if it could be found.

With the confidence of a completed 100-mile race, solid training, and the wonderful optimism of youth, Tim tackled other races and learned some things, sometimes the hard way. When things weren't working at his second Western States, Tim desperately tried to initiate change. That didn't work. Putting it delicately, the output exceeded the input. His weight dropped, and he stopped for well over an hour. His father was pacing him and saw a different race than the year before. Grimly hanging on, Tim concluded that run in 22:53, good for 50th overall. No doubt he spent many training runs after that trying to figure out what happened so he would not repeat it. More work needed to be done.

A year later at his third Western States, Tim took almost an hour off of his best finish time, placing 30th overall with 21:04. In 1984, Tim couldn't toe the start line because he had not won a lottery entry for the popular race. Other races and training filled the time after work and family. A return to Western States in 1985 found a slightly different Tim. I would suggest a break-through Tim—10th overall with a finish time of 18:42. At subsequent Western States, times would be slightly greater than that until 1989 when 30-year-old Tim had another breakthrough, pushing to finish in the seventeenth hour with 17:06, good for 2nd place.

Tim kept running, working and trying to balance his many interests while annually finishing the Western States race.

In 1992, a friend told him about a dream he had of Tim winning Western States. In the three years prior, Tim's race results didn't reflect confidence in that outcome, having dropped from second to third to fourth with comparable finish times. The race continued to draw the attention of some of the best ultrarunners around, making the field more and more competitive every year. Of course, there would be weather and race-day trail conditions to deal with, too. Yet, Tim had put in solid training, knew the course having raced it 10 times before, frequently trained on its trails (that were almost in his backyard), and had many racing experiences in a variety of conditions. Come race day, the trail was in great shape, and the temperatures didn't climb too high. Staying out of the early lead, Tim picked his way to the front, and midway through the race, took over the lead. Tim kept the lead to the end, living out his friend's dream and making the cover of *Ultrarunning* magazine, the ultrarunning equivalent of a cereal box cover. His 11th finish at Western States, first overall in 16:54. A champion at last.

Conditions for the 1993 edition of Western States were very different: snow in the high country and heat with temperatures over 100 degrees Fahrenheit. Race results reflected these conditions with slower overall times and a lower finish rate. Tim's finish time would be over an hour slower than the year before, 17:56, but good for 2nd overall. Tim would go on to notch three wins in the next three years. Ann Trason placed second to Tim twice. In 1994, 46 minutes separated them, but in the hottest Western States, the 1995 race margin would be just 6 minutes. In 1996, Tim again finished first overall and notched his 15th finish under 24 hours at the race.

RUNNING TO EXTREMES

In 1997, Tim would place second behind the race winner who would set a new course record. A year later, Tim would notch his fifth overall victory. In 1999, Tim would come in second to a rookie, Scott Jurek, who would go on to win the next seven Western States. Tim continued to run Western States through 2006 when he made a conscious decision to make it his last. Seems that it was more about doing something else than it was about not doing it again. 25 sub-24-hour finishes, 5 wins, and 15 top-ten finishes—a great legacy with a great race.

But Tim didn't turn his back on the Western States race. It turns out he has been giving back to the sport and the race for a very long time. On the Western States board of trustees since 1996, Tim is very involved—trail maintenance, rule and organizational changes, holding several offices. In fact, it was Tim's name as president of the board on the notification to runners in 2008 that the race was cancelled due to wildfires and their effects. Nor did he step away from running. Tim had enjoyed a variety of races he had used for training, so he continued with those. He has more than 30 finishes at the 50-mile race American River, as just one example. All total, Tim has done well over 200 marathons and ultramarathons, winning many and setting numerous course records along the way.

Back in the day, Tim tracked his workouts and results with his highest weekly mileage at 80 to 85 miles. Despite not running competitively in high school or college, Tim figured it out one race at a time. He was constantly making adjustments to get the results he wanted and the balance he needed. He and his friends refer to the "domestic tranquility index" that seems to measure the balance of many factors and that must be in harmony for the best results, whether it be the results at home, work, or play. Possibly this balance may have helped Tim from getting burned out or suffering from overuse. It definitely pushed him to make efficient use of his training time.

Cross-training—biking swimming, hiking—is now a bigger part of his training schedule. Lots of variety while he still runs three to four times a week. Tim bikes to and from work more days than not, as he has done for years. It seems that his friends had a good chuckle over his first mountain bike ride, but Tim adapted quickly, and the laughs were silenced. Tim strung some of these talents together for a good finish at Ironman Wisconsin in 2009, earning him a spot at the 2010 Ironman Championships in Kona, Hawaii. Tim suggests that his best time running doesn't include a clock, but instead a challenge. His voice amps up a bit when he talks about running the Tahoe Rim Trail, a winter crossing on the Western States trail, a run from Carson City to Sacramento, fast packing through the Sierras, the "Ice Cream Sandwich" runs, or hooking up with friends for an endurance bike ride. Tim mirrors a supportive environment that he so appreciated, and he extends it to friends and soon-to-be friends. Parts of his weeks are devoted to introducing roadrunners to trail running. Showing them where the trail is, discussing trail etiquette, pointing out the equipment demands, and simply running with them. Since his first win at Western States, Tim ably took up the mantle of representing the sport and being a role model. One of the best ways is to simply have fun, which is what Tim has been doing.

There were a few occasions when Tim did not finish (DNF) a planned race, portraying their rare occasions now as more regrets than disasters. Sometimes things just don't come together or the course finds a weakness. Sometimes mistakes were made, like too much racing or training leading up to an event. Lessons were learned. I tend to think we would all agree that settling for a shorter distance when a knee got tweaked mid-race was better than risking further damage. Achilles and plantar fasciitis issues are also not foreign to Tim, but they are properly managed and definitely not chronic—another benefit of balance.

RUNNING TO **EXTREMES**

Tim credits his mom for the traditional Western States pre-race meal of spaghetti and meatballs, salad, French bread, and brownies with family all around to provide both nutritional and emotional support for the event ahead. Like many, Tim was always making adjustments to balance his goals and dreams with his life priorities. His family supported his running in a variety of ways, but most importantly by just being there. In the early years, family members helped out as both pacers crew. Tim reflects that a good run at Western States meant finishing early enough for a shower and reading a bedtime story to his boys before putting them to bed that night. As his race times decreased, it's likely that the amount of time he actually saw his family during the race declined, but he still enjoyed their support every step down the trail.

Ever appreciative of the opportunities and support, Tim is very involved in many activities that provide that. Active on the Western States board, he hangs around to see those late finishers at Western States, getting a real charge out of encouraging them, congratulating them, and sharing their personal victory. His streak of 50-mile finishes continues at American River, logging the same finish time as one of his sons. He speaks fondly of trail maintenance weekends that include working on improvements with a friendly group that brings along some adult beverages, has pizza delivered, and just maybe shares some old-fashioned storytelling. It occurs to me these occasions might be the time to get the real colorful stories and harrowing episodes that Tim doesn't think to call attention to.

Grounded by family and friends, Tim's exploration of ultrarunning accompanied by fun and discovery come out easily in conversation. So easily that I was almost convinced that I was talking to anybody, say an average Joe. But I wasn't. I was talking to Tim Twietmeyer, a guy who's going to have to work a whole lot harder to just be average.

TIM TWIETMEYER

RUNNING TO **EXTREMES**

CHAPTER 12

HELEN KLEIN

HELEN KLEIN

Do you think it's possible for an 8 x 10 sheet of paper to completely change your life? Do fate, destiny, and karma truly exist? From my perspective, the answer to all of these questions can be summarized in one word: Yes.

An 8 x 10 sheet of paper changed the life of my wife, Helen. Let me explain.

Once upon a time, Helen had never done anything athletic in her entire life. After reading the next chapter, that sentence alone may be the most difficult one to comprehend in this entire book chronicling athletes who pushed the limits of human endurance. At a point when most people are contemplating retirement and spoiling their grandchildren, Helen's life took a dramatic turn—a turn that transformed her into arguably the greatest senior master marathon, ultramarathon, and endurance athlete of all time.

By virtue of Helen's incredible athletic accomplishments, the two of us have had the good fortune to have been invited to participate in many races throughout the United States and all over the world.

In time, Helen's athletic involvement branched out into many other areas: race director, motivational speaker, middle school track coach, and mentor to marathon and ultramarathon runners of all shapes and sizes. Helen had quite a career.

As for that 8 x 10 sheet of paper, you'll read about it in the following pages.

It is my pleasure to write this introduction to the chapter dedicated to Helen Klein, an amazing athlete, a wonderful person, and the love of my life.

–Norm Klein

RUNNING TO EXTREMES

LATE BLOOMER

By Norm Klein

We were living in the small town of Hopkinsville, Kentucky. The year was 1978. Helen was 55 years young at the time. I was a practicing oral and maxillofacial surgeon; Helen assisted me in my office as a nurse. A local bank was sponsoring a race—the first ever staged in town. An orthopedic surgeon who lived on our street was running six miles a day at the time and was always encouraging me to run with him. I had absolutely no interest in running.

Then one day, Helen and I came home from the office, and there was a flyer for the race in our mailbox. There was a note attached to it saying I had 10 weeks to get ready for this. It wasn't signed, but I knew whom it was from. There were two events: a 10-mile and a 10-kilometer run. Never the one to back down from a challenge, I said to Helen, "We ought to do this. You can run the 10K, and I'll do the 10-miler." This was a time when there weren't any women in town running, and Helen was too embarrassed to go into the street wearing a pair of shorts. We had some acreage on our property, so I hopped on the lawn mower and cut the grass really low, making a fifth-of-a-mile loop for her to train. It was July in Kentucky, and the temperature was regularly in the 90s with 90 percent humidity. Helen ran three loops and wondered how on earth she was ever going to run 6.2 miles. I urged her to run 7 miles the next weekend, 8 the next, then 9, and we could run 10 miles together the weekend after that. And so we did.

During the race, the sag wagon (an ambulance to assist those in distress) followed us the entire way. We finished dead last. But we finished. There were 50 runners in the race: 46 men and 4 women—Helen and three high school cross-country runners. Not surprisingly, Helen won the 40 and over age group. She won a trophy, had her photograph taken, and earned a first-place T-shirt. Little did we know at the time this would be, as they say, the start of something big.

In 1979, I decided to run a marathon, hoping that someday I could qualify to run Boston. I ran the Chicago Marathon, and Helen accompanied me to the race. She was so excited seeing all the runners and decided she, too, would like to run a marathon. So in 1980, at the age of 56, Helen and I went to Florida where she would run the Miamithon Marathon. She finished in 4:43, and, interesting to note, 23 years later at the age of 80, she ran a 4:31 and broke the world record for her age group by 39 minutes.

After several more marathons, it was time to move up to the ultra. By this time, Helen had also made a commitment to run a marathon (or longer) in every state. We saw an ad for a 50-mile race in Mount Vernon, Washington. The race was conducted on a five-mile loop, so I decided to try it. Helen had the intention of running five laps and adding an extra 1.2 miles so she could add another state to her résumé. After five laps she was feeling pretty good and decided to run another lap. This would continue for another four laps, and just like that, she ran 50 miles and completed her first ultra. She admitted afterward she was no more tired than she was after running a marathon.

Just prior to the Mount Vernon race we were in St. Louis for a marathon, and I saw a runner with a Hawaii Ironman T-shirt. I spent a great deal of time talking to him about the event and decided to make it my next challenge. In February of 1982, I went to Hawaii for the Ironman. Helen accompanied me, and (surprise!) she said she would like to try it as well. She couldn't swim very well, so she took swimming lessons from the high school swim coach, but it made me wonder how swimming laps in our 36-foot pool (155 laps to the mile) would translate into swimming

RUNNING TO EXTREMES

2.4 miles in the ocean. Besides that, she hadn't ridden a bicycle in almost 50 years, let alone a 12-speed. She bought a bike, and the first day on it proved to be a disaster. She fell three times just getting out of the driveway. The owner of the local bike shop came by and gave her a lesson on how to get on and off the bike and how to use the brakes and derailleurs. After that she was fine, and that October, we went to Hawaii, where Helen successfully finished her first Ironman competition.

In 1983, Helen expressed an interest in running the Western States Endurance Run—100 miles through the Sierra Nevada mountain range. With no hills to train on in Kentucky, Helen opted to test her endurance by running in Ray Krolewicz's 24-hour run in South Carolina. A torn hamstring prevented me from running, but Helen ran in weather best described as a nightmare. There was a torrential downpour and severe winds for eight hours. One section of the track was under several inches of water for much of the race. Helen persisted and finished 100 miles in 26:41; she was the only woman in the race.

Three months later we were off to California for Western States. That year there was an all-time record snowfall in the Sierra Nevada Mountains. The first 30 miles of the race was on a five-foot snow pack. Slipping, sliding, and falling became the norm. I was fortunate to finish, but Helen encountered some real difficulty. Water had to be helicoptered to the first aid station at mile 10, where Helen had to wait 17 minutes to hydrate since the next aid station was another seven miles away. As a result, she missed the time cutoff at Devil's Thumb (mile 47.8) by nine minutes. She came to the finish line to see me finish and said, "I'll never try this again." However, on the flight home, she changed her tune: "Maybe if I lived there [California] and could train on the hills, I could finish."

I gave her comment considerable thought and decided that maybe it was time for a career change, not to mention a geographical change. So four months later, I sold my practice, we packed all of our belongings, and we moved to the Sacramento area so we could train in the mountains. I had no idea what I would do to earn a living, but I figured what the hell. I was confident I could find something. The move proved to be all that Helen needed. In 1984 at the age of 61 and again in 1985 at the age of 62, Helen finished Western States.

We heard that Western States was looking for a new race director, so we applied for the position (as co-race directors). We were selected in December of 1985 to direct the 1986 event. We would go on to direct the Western States Endurance Run—the Super Bowl of 100-mile mountain trail races—for 14 years. That first year we wondered to ourselves if we were up to the challenge.

Our dear friend, Dick Collins, suggested to Helen that she should try a multi-day race. In November of 1986, Helen flew to New York to run the Sri Chimnoy five-day race. The women's course record was 279 miles; as her goal was to break the record, Helen stopped at 280 miles. In 1987, Tom Green, an ultrarunner from Maryland, decided to run the Old Dominion 100, Western States, Leadville 100, and Wasatch 100 over a span of 11 weeks. He was successful and became the first person to complete what is now known as the Grand Slam of 100-mile trail runs. This, of course, put a bug in Helen's ear, so in 1989, Helen, along with Suzie Tiebault from California, Lou Peyton from Arkansas, and Marge Adelman from Colorado, decided to do what Tom did two years earlier. All four of them were successful.

To give some perspective to what these four women accomplished, the Boston Marathon is considered by some as a difficult marathon because there is 1,500 feet of elevation change. In the four races constituting the Grand Slam, there is 186,000 feet of elevation change. That's like going from sea level to the summit of Mount Everest (29,000 feet) and back—three times.

RUNNING TO EXTREMES

The other three women then decided to run the Angeles Crest 100-miler, so Helen decided she would as well. Helen, Suzie, and Lou were successful; Marge was unable to finish. As for Helen, she finished five 100-mile trail runs in 16 weeks—not too shabby for a 66-year-old woman.

After Helen's success at the five-day race in New York, we decided to hold a multi-day race in Sacramento where runners could run either 24, 48, 72, or 144 hours. In 1991, we held the race on a one-mile loop in Gibson Ranch, a county park in Sacramento. Much to our surprise, runners from around the world came to participate. Also to our surprise, the temperatures plummeted to 14 and 17 degrees Fahrenheit the second and third nights, respectively. Despite the two coldest temperatures ever recorded in Sacramento, very few runners withdrew, and the race turned out to be a huge success. Helen was 68 years old and managed to run 340 miles. Then only three months later she set a world record by running 109.5 miles in the Redwood Empire 24-hour run in Santa Rosa, California.

Our friend, Ian Javes, from Australia held a six-day race in his hometown of Caboolture, Queensland, Australia. Ian had run all of our six-day races at Gibson Ranch, so Helen decided to return the favor. In 1992, we flew to Australia, and Helen ran 354.9 miles in six days. Then a mere three months later—at age 70—she broke her own world record at Gibson Ranch by running 373 miles in six days.

One of Helen's most difficult events occurred when she was 72. We were both invited to participate in the Marathon Des Sables, a 150-mile stage race across the Sahara Desert in Morocco. The only thing provided to the runners was water, so you had to carry everything you needed for five days (food, clothing, cooking supplies, medical supplies). Imagine having to run while carrying a 25-pound pack in 110-degree temperatures. In the desert. Unfortunately I broke my leg six miles into the first day, so Helen was forced to continue on her own. Women had to compete against the men as only one award was given in each age group. Helen was the only woman to win her age group, having beaten all of the 70-year-old men in the process.

Perhaps Helen's greatest challenge took place only 12 days after her victory in Morocco. Helen was selected to be a member of a five-person team competing in the Eco Challenge, a multisport (running, mountaineering, mountain biking, canoeing, white water rafting, and horseback riding) event covering 370 miles across Utah's Moab Desert. Helen had never done any technical climbing, so she took three lessons from a 19-year-old student at the University of California-Davis in an old two-story gymnasium. He taught Helen how to climb, repel, and cross a Tyrolean Traverse. Since she had never done any canoeing or horseback riding, she took two lessons apiece to learn how. A friend came and gave her a couple of lessons on a mountain bike.

The rules for the Eco Challenge were simple: If one person dropped out, the entire team was disqualified. The next oldest person on Helen's team was a 42-year-old man. A film crew from *Dateline NBC* was there, and they followed Helen's team the entire way, so Helen knew she just had to finish. Going into the final event—a 50-mile canoe paddle to the finish—the team was in 13th place. They made a wrong turn and went five miles out of the way on the river. Of the 50 teams that started, only 21 finished. Helen's team, Operation Smile, finished in 18th place. They raised $40,000 for a charity that helps to provide surgery for disfigured children. They finished the event in 9 days and 10 hours; Helen estimates they got only eight hours of sleep during that time.

Helen ran her last 100-mile trail run at the Rocky Raccoon 100-miler at the Huntsville State Park in Huntsville, Texas, at the age of 75. Several months later we ran the Shadow of the Giants 50K Trail Run near Yosemite. Five of us were running together with Helen in the lead, followed by two other women, and I was bringing up the rear. Helen was focused on keeping her eyes on the trail and didn't see a tree that had fallen diagonally over the trail. She hit it head on and instantly crumbled to the ground. When she sat up, there was blood gushing from a two-inch gash to her forehead. I always carried a first aid kit in my backpack, so I tended to the wound with some gauze. I couldn't stop the bleeding, so as a last resort, I took off my T-shirt and wrapped it around her head like a tourniquet. The bleeding ultimately stopped, and when we crossed the finish line, I changed the dressing. The accident occurred at mile 24, and amazingly, Helen ran those last seven miles at a faster pace than she had been running earlier in the race.

After the race, Helen said she was hungry, so we, along with two friends traveling with us, stopped at a restaurant before heading back for our three-and-a-half hour drive to Sacramento. You can probably imagine the reaction from the patrons and servers at the restaurant when we walked in, Helen with a bloody dressing wrapped around her head. We finally got home around 10 p.m., I sat Helen down in the kitchen and carefully cleaned her wound, injected some local anesthesia, and sutured the laceration with 10 stitches. Helen Klein: One tough lady.

Helen continued running marathons and ultras, and, in 2002, at the age of 80, broke the world record for her age group in the marathon by 39 minutes at the California International Marathon. The publicity she received as a result of it brought invitations to marathons all over the country. This would continue for five more years until, once again, at the California International Marathon, she broke the world record for women age 80 and over (Helen was 85) by running it in 5:49, bettering the existing world record by over 64 minutes.

Just three short months later, an interesting thing happened at the Napa Valley Marathon. Helen was off to an incredible start, and when I saw her at mile 21, she was on pace to lower her world record by at least

30 minutes. I hurried to the finish line to see the historic moment, and I waited...and waited...but she wasn't coming. Finally, when she came across the finish line, she was covered in blood from head to toe. It seems that at mile 23 she came around a corner, and a huge gust of wind blew her into a rose bush where she became literally impaled. She tore herself loose—tearing off huge pieces of tissue from her arms and legs in the process—and in spite of the mishap still finished in 5:36, lowering her world record by another 13 minutes.

After 93 marathons and 143 ultras, Helen decided it was time to retire. She still goes out every morning for a five-mile run, and on weekends she still runs hills.

Looking back over Helen's fabulous career, I wondered what enabled a 55-year-young woman who had never done anything athletically to accomplish what she did over those 30 amazing years. I attribute it to the code Helen lived by: the Three Ds:

> Determination—Establish a goal, pick an event, and work hard to accomplish that goal.
>
> Dedication—Dedicate yourself to that goal and train no matter what the weather may be or what other obstacles may stand in your way.
>
> Discipline—During an event, no matter how tired physically or mentally you may be, press on because eventually you probably will be able to work through it.

So now I ask you: Did an 8 x 10 sheet of paper change our lives?

You bet it did.

RUNNING TO **EXTREMES**

CHAPTER 13

ERIC CLIFTON

ERIC CLIFTON

When I was asked to write the introduction to Eric's chapter, I thought it would be fairly easy. I was wrong...

Thinking about Eric's accomplishments and my memories running, talking, and being his friend made me realize something that takes me out of my comfort zone. Eric Clifton is the most influential person in my life. Having come to that conclusion in my heart makes me uncomfortable because I think of all the other people in my life: my brothers, parents, relatives, and even my own daughter. Of course they all play a huge part in who I am as a person and a soldier. But Eric has forged my character more than any one person.

Eric is the single most values-driven person I have ever met. He always does the hard right when the easy wrong would be the most painless choice. Simply put, he does what is right even when only he would know if he didn't. He is compassionate, thoughtful, and the most competitive person I have ever been friends with. I have found myself in some pretty tough situations as a soldier at war—times when I feared the safety of my teammates or myself might be at risk from injury or death. During those times, it takes compassion and a thoughtful approach to think and not act too quickly or aggressively. Often I would ask myself, what would Eric do? Eric is the metric of morals and ethics that I use in my life.

Eric is a warrior at heart—a fiercely competitive person. He has a unique approach to running that I learned when we trained and raced together: run fast and hard, all the time. Many runners have a plan or race strategy that involves different times to push or conserve effort, but not Eric; it is wide open or broke. I respect that approach because it follows a logical path for me: Keep it simple and run. The all or nothing approach works for Eric, as he has created some of the most amazing artwork of any artist I've ever met. Eric once told me that as runners we would one day be long gone, but people will look back at the art we made through our performances. That had a very profound impact on me; I have applied that logic to many aspects of my life—not just running! It has helped me when I'm not being a good person, because I think, is this a piece of art I want to be remembered for? Not being a good father or a good husband? Of course there have been many times I create some hideous art—that's all part of being human.

When you read about Eric's running accomplishments, I'm sure you will be amazed! His determination and fortitude inspire at every level. What I want to make sure you know is that his running is nothing compared to his character and values or to the man himself. Eric—like everyone—is not perfect, but he is the closest thing to it that I have ever found. Just don't believe him if he tells you that you don't need an extra water bottle and a headlamp! Those stories require a whole other book—a survival book. Enjoy his chapter!

–Mike Morton

LONG LASTING

By David Corfman

Many of us aspire to have a rewarding avocation in a sport, whether it is running, golf, tennis, or cycling. Some of us even aspire to turn professional. Some athletes can do well in multiple sports, even reaching elite status in multiple disciplines. Very few can reach a high level of performance and then maintain it for years or even decades. Those select athletes add a new dimension to the prefix "ultra."

Eric Clifton has reached the highest level of performance in multiple sports. He has excelled in road marathons, triathlons, distance cycling, and, most prominently, ultramarathons. Yet, it would be all for naught if he couldn't maintain a high level of performance. Eric's greatest pride is in the longevity he has demonstrated for more than three decades.

Career One: Road Racing

Eric's running career started out rather understated. In fact, it was practically non-existent in his early years. He was psyched out from running high school cross-country when a braggart told him they ran 10 miles per day for training. In hindsight, judging from the team's lackluster performance, Eric realized 10 miles a day had to be an exaggeration! He competed in the long-distance events in track in his senior year, with modest results to show for it. There were very few signs of the running ability that was yet to be discovered.

As Eric entered college in 1976, distance running was entering its boom years. He joined a running club near his Greensboro, North Carolina, campus and started entering road races. He immediately set his sights on the marathon distance and ran his first one in 1977, the Greensboro Marathon. Once hooked on marathons, the ultimate prize for Eric was qualifying for and running the Boston Marathon. Back then, when Eric was still a young lad, he had to run a 2:50 to qualify. It took him three years to reach that plateau, but reach it he did.

But qualifying for Boston and running it are two different things. After running a qualifying time, Eric would not take the opportunity to experience Boylston Street for another 16 years. Another sport piqued his interest, consuming his time and racing calendar.

Career Two: Triathlons

Every kid owned a bicycle growing up. Most kids got some swimming instruction, as well. Combine those two interests with a budding running career, and a triathlete is born. Eric had immediate success in the multi-disciplines of triathlons. Just as the marathon has Boston as its ultimate destination, the triathlon has Kona. Eric qualified for and competed in the Ironman World Championships four times, his highest overall finish being 11th (1984).

Success at such a high level in a grueling sport is meaningless if you aren't able to enjoy it. Eric didn't like the direction the sport was headed—high entry fees, overcrowded races, and rampant cheating. Note this was in the mid-1980s (entry fees for Ironman events are even more exorbitant today). But the Ironman triathlons introduced Eric to the world of athletic events that took longer than three or four hours to complete.

Career Three: Ultracycling

This was a short-lived career for Eric, but he was still quite successful at it. Ultracycling involves cycling long distances with predetermined routes or durations. In his single ultracycling race, he qualified for RAAM (Race Across America), which is ultracycling's Boston Marathon. While Eric had crewed for his wife's four starts at RAAM, Eric never started RAAM himself. After she fell during the 1986 RAAM and broke her neck, a friend told him about another sport—a sport done on trails, and one Eric ultimately fell in love with.

Career Four: Ultramarathons

Eric actually ran his first ultramarathon race in 1982, a 50-mile road race where he did everything wrong, and his knee paid the price. It took a long time to put that memory behind him, but Eric became energized once again when he discovered that ultras were also run on trails. With all the arrogance and ignorance of a young athlete who had tasted success in multiple sports, Eric signed up for his first 50-mile Mountain Masochist Trail Run in 1986. The reality of running a tough 50-mile race hit him early, and he suffered through the middle portion of the race. But an aid station break that included a soda brought him back to life, and his strong sixth-place finish got him hooked on his favorite sport. (Eric would go on to complete 10 MMTRs, winning twice. More on those unique finishes later.)

His next race was the Stone Mountain (Georgia) 50-mile race on roads the same year, finishing in 6:16 for his first ultramarathon win. It was obvious that Eric had considerable ability to run long distances; he also had a real calling for the trails. Just like every other sport he had been involved with, Eric quickly reached for the pinnacle. The Western States

RUNNING TO EXTREMES

Endurance Run, the Boston of ultramarathons, is the original 100-mile race. He qualified for Western States with his 50-mile race and started the 1987 edition of the classic.

But in a sport that rewards experience, Eric's neophyte standing cost him a finish. Eric suffered from nausea in that race. It spooked him, and he failed to finish. Since then he has discovered how to throw up and keep running. It wasn't until his fifth attempt at the 100-mile distance, the 1989 Vermont 100 Endurance Run, that he finally finished. Despite getting off course for over six miles, he not only finished, but he also won the event!

While his 15:48 was a tremendous time at Vermont, the true breakthrough was the experience he had while racing on those White Mountain trails. From his Sep/Oct 2004 *Marathon and Beyond* article, Eric wrote, "That is when I felt in my heart the two primary reasons why I run: I run to exceed my perceived limits, to do better than I think I can. Even more important, I learned to run without fear and with bliss. Because I had run an extra six miles, if I finished the race I would have run more than 100 miles. Even better, I discovered the joy of running with ease at a seemingly unstoppable fast pace. It really was all good."

Ultrarunner of the Year

The euphoria from his 1989 Vermont 100 race (but not necessarily his win) carried Eric the next several years to great success on the circuit. He defended his Vermont 100 win three straight years and conquered Western States, earning the coveted silver buckle (sub-24-hour finish). Along with Vermont, Eric won three other 100-mile races in 1992, the first runner ever to do such a feat in a single year. For that he was named the 1992 Ultrarunner of the Year.

Four finishes, especially wins, at the 100-mile distance would be a great career for most ultramarathoners. But for Eric, it was only a single year that would serve up greater things. It was time to write his name in the record books.

The Need for Speed...and Course Records

100-mile races require great endurance. 10Ks, when run properly, require speed. To perform well at a marathon requires lots of both speed and endurance. Eric continued to dabble in races at all distances and, in 1994, ran his personal best at the marathon distance. He ran the Charlotte Observer Marathon in 2:31, not a particularly fast time by today's elite standards. In fact, it wasn't until 1999 when Eric would finally win his first marathon, 22 years after running his first "mary," as Eric calls them.

Eric's speed manifested itself in longer distances, but he never had the blazing speed of a top marathoner. His fast times came from how he ran the longer distances. He would go out fast and remain fast for as long as possible. He would run trail races with the speed of a road race. He would blast through aid stations. He wouldn't hold himself back, and course records started to fall.

In 1994, Eric set the course record at the famed JFK 50-Mile. His 5:46 that day was a record that would stand for 17 years. Eric breaks down the JFK 50-Mile into three parts: the technical 15 miles on the Appalachian Trail to Weaverton, a flat marathon on the C&O towpath, and then about 8 miles of rolling roads to the finish line. When he set the long-lasting record, Eric laid down a 2:52 for the marathon-length middle section. That's fast, but it means he ran the other tougher 24 miles in 2:54. He started fast that day, not holding himself back. That was his style.

RUNNING TO EXTREMES

Eric kept up the speed and intensity for even longer distances when he set both a course record and a personal best for the 100-mile distance at Rocky Raccoon in 1996, finishing in 13:16. That course record would stand for 15 years. Eric would set course records at Mount Rushmore 100, Old Dominion 100, Arkansas Traveler 100, Badwater 135, and Uwharrie 40-miler, among others. Some of those records still stand today.

Running on the Sun

The documentary, *Running on the Sun,* about the 1999 edition of the Badwater ultramarathon showed one of Eric's most famous races. However, even Eric admits it wasn't a very good race for him. A couple months earlier, a pundit posted on the Ultra listserv bulletin board that Eric would run well early, but eventually fail to finish and not be a factor in the race. Tell Eric he can't do something, and he will prove you wrong. That was all the motivation he needed.

But the Badwater win wasn't as easy as the documentary showed. The first 42 miles to Stovepipe Wells went fine, just as the pundit had suggested, but it was difficult for Eric after that, going up and over Townes Pass in the oppressive heat and headwinds and then across Panamint Springs at night. Then, in the early hours of the next morning, getting over Father Crowley's Crossing was a period when he had to slow down to a dawdling mosey. In the documentary, featured runner Nick Palazzo was cranky to his crew when they couldn't get him his much-needed soup fast enough. Eric had his own energy issues at just about the same point on the course when he ran out of chocolate milk.

With the help of his crew and a new supply of chocolate milk, Eric was revived and ran through Lone Pine as the leader to the cheers of all tens of spectators. (It's not a big town.) Power hiking up to the trail portals of Mount Whitney to stay ahead of a hard-charging Gabriel Flores, Eric earned the win and, at the time, a course record.

The Jester

Eric Clifton took his running and racing seriously but has never taken himself *too* seriously. He wears bright running tights and uses joke pseudonyms at shorter distances. His favorite pseudonym is jester wag, which literally means "joke joke." Thus the moniker, "the Jester," has stuck. Even his e-mail signature is "jester," along with a giant emoticon of a runner.

His tights have a more modest genesis. When Eric started racing triathlons, a tri suit cost about $65, which was more than Eric wanted to spend. Being from North Carolina where most Lycra was made, Eric could easily find cheap material with lots of variety. So he got his mother to teach him how to sew, and he started making himself tri suits and later tights and vests.

As he became successful at ultramarathons, he went from dark horse to being the target of the other frontrunners. Why settle for black or dark blue tights when you can go loud and flashy? That was more Eric's style. Look for some of his running pictures, and you will be amused by his fashion sense. His running was serious, but his choice of running attire was anything but.

His Longevity

One area in which Eric has had few equals is his longevity. Runners all hope to be running for a few decades, but to be able to compete *and win* for over a quarter century (wins from 1986 to 2014, and hopefully

RUNNING TO EXTREMES

beyond) puts him in a category by himself. In fact, his 19-year streak (through 2005) with at least one ultramarathon win is listed as one of the longest such streaks.

Eric finished the Mountain Masochist Trail Run 50-mile race 10 times. In 1990, he won in his fastest time ever at that race, finishing in 7:02:46 but collapsing at the finish line, disappointed with his performance that he didn't break the magical seven-hour mark. He was able to keep up this level of performance throughout all his Mountain Masochist races, taking almost all top-10 positions in his 10 finishes (although "trading" a fourth-place finish for a second win). Yes, he came in first twice, second, third, fifth, sixth, seventh, eighth, ninth, and tenth. That is consistently high performance.

New ultrarunners splash onto the scene, make their mark, and then disappear due to injury or whatnot. Do an Internet search for "David Riddle" for a prime example. When talking about the next great runner, Eric thinks of David Horton's favorite line, "Well, let's see what they are doing five years from now."

Eric is proud of his running achievements but accepts that each of his records will eventually be broken. He takes more pride in maintaining his ability to run at a very high level for as long as he has, running races his way: with heart.

Racing Philosophy

Eric Clifton's running philosophy has been criticized due to his many DNFs (Did Not Finish). While it is true that Eric has dropped out of more races than many ultrarunners have even entered (currently 69 DNFs to go with his 60 wins), it is because he pushes the envelope at each race. Eric doesn't race against his rivals; he simply runs each race as if it were his last. If a rival helped him focus his attention to running his best, then that usually worked out better for both of them.

One friendly rivalry decades ago was with David Horton. The year Eric won Ultrarunner of the Year (1992), they raced against each other seven times, with Horton beating him in four of those races. In 1990, David was running the JFK 50-Mile in second place and was ahead of Eric with less than two miles to go. Up ahead was the first-place runner, going very slowly. The three lead runners were in sight of one another. David's pacer, his son, urged him to catch the lead runner, but David was focused on only one goal: beating his friend Eric Clifton. David beat Eric that day. His rivals may have raced against him, but Eric raced against himself.

While David Horton and most ultramarathoners would run cautiously and earn a win, Eric would rather "fail" in races in order to challenge himself and the course. But was it really failing if he just didn't win? Winning by running conservatively meant very little to Eric. It was a race, and it called for giving it your all.

Contrary to Badwater Ben's comments in *Running on the Sun*, Eric would not DNF just to save himself for another race. The great runner, Steve Prefontaine, said, "To give anything less than your best, is to sacrifice the gift." Eric personified that statement; he would go out as hard as he could for as long as he could until he would win or DNF. If he DNF'ed, it was because he was exhausted. If he won, then the course record was often in jeopardy.

Places, finishes, and course records don't matter much to Eric. He looks for magic in his races, those times when he doesn't have to *make* himself run hard, but rather can *let* himself run hard. We all look for those mystical races ourselves, and when they happen, we can hold on tight to those experiences with no regrets that we didn't give it our best.

Run from your heart—for decades. Like Eric Clifton.

RUNNING TO **EXTREMES**

CHAPTER 14

ED ETTINGHAUSEN

I met Ed Ettinghausen in December of 2010 at a 72-hour race called Across the Years. This was my very first multi-day race, and I honestly did not know what to expect. As the race started, I noticed this very tall man wearing the largest cowboy hat I have ever seen and wondered who this crazy guy could be. I wondered even more as he swapped it out with a jester hat later in the race. I then realized that I not only did not know what to expect at this race, but that I was surrounded by a very unique group of people, including this man who definitely stood out in the crowd. What I did not realize at the time was how amazing this group of people was and how fortunate I was to be running with them. Ed, otherwise known as the Jester, was one of the people who unknowingly helped me come to that realization.

The Jester has done some pretty amazing things wearing that jester hat, like completing Badwater more than once and running 40 races of 100 miles or more in one year. However, one thing that always stands out to me about the Jester is not his amazing athletic accomplishments, but rather the amount of time that he always has for others. He greets everyone with a smile, a handshake, or a high five. I have often heard him offer helpful advice to other runners. He is a down-to-earth guy and one of the most approachable people that I have met in the world of multi-day endurance events. And it goes without saying: The man is one heck of an athlete.

Since my first Across the Years, I have seen the Jester and his wonderful wife, Martha, every December, as we both seem to return to that same multi-day race in Arizona. I am always glad to see him there; it just wouldn't be the same without the sound of bells and his bright presence. I look forward to his high five each time runners change direction during the race.

Those high fives are important to all of us.

–Vikena Yutz

RUNNING TO **EXTREMES**

LATHER, RINSE, REPEAT, REPEAT, REPEAT...

By David Corfman

Many of us have run a marathon, or even multiple marathons, in a single year. There are some runners who take running marathons to an extreme—Marathon Maniacs club is full of examples—where you find running a couple marathons in a single weekend is the norm. Ed Ettinghausen took running marathons to a new level, setting a world record of running 135 marathons in 365 days.

But this book is about the limits of human endurance. You would have read in this book about 50 marathons in 50 days or running across America in 52 days (averaging 58 miles per day). Ed would have to do something that really pushes the limits of human endurance to be included in this book. Flip the pages and read how Ed fulfills that requirement, earning his second world record in the process.

Modest Beginnings to Marathoning

DC: When did you start running? You ran your first marathon in high school before marathons were popular or even well known.

EE: *Growing up, I went to a couple of very small parochial schools that had no organized sporting competitions of any kind, let alone any cross-country or track-and-field programs. The only organized running we did was in P.E. class and once a year at track-and-field day. In high school, I started running on my own. I read everything about marathons that I could get my hands on, devouring every issue of Runner's World from front to back. It was the beginning of the nation's first "jogging" craze,* and I read books by Jim Fixx, Dr. Sheehan, Dr. Mirkin, and Dr. Ken Cooper. I was bitten by the bug.

In August 1979, at the age of 16, I ran in my first organized race—a small 3-mile fun run—and placed third overall. From all the reading I had done, I gleaned what I could to put together a marathon training program, and at the age of 17, I ran my second organized race—a marathon. It was the Sri Chinmoy Marathon in San Francisco. [It no longer exists.] I ran it like any headstrong, red-blooded 17-year-old would and went out way too fast. Somehow, I willed myself across the finish line in 3:10.

If I was smitten by the running bug before, I was now completely devoured by it. One month later, I ran the San Francisco Marathon. In a nine-month span, starting from my first marathon adventure, I ran a total of five marathons, with a PR of 3:01:18 at age 18 at the third annual Napa Valley Marathon.

I had attempted to run the L.A. Marathon in 1994, but because I hadn't trained properly with any kind of base, my knees became quite pained. Even though I blasted out at a sub-3 pace, by mile 3, the knee pain caused me to slow quite a bit, and before I could even reach the four-mile marker, I was reduced to a slow walk. I turned around, walking the opposite direction of the myriad oncoming runners, like an ill-fated salmon, swimming upstream to its ultimate end.

After that experience, many people "in the know" told me that I had ruined my knees from the heavy training mileage and those five silly marathons as a teenager. I believed them and didn't attempt to run another marathon for the next 15 years.

RUNNING TO EXTREMES

DC: That's a long break from running marathons. How did your return to running marathons go?

EE: *So from March 1981 until March 2009, I completed a single marathon—walking the L.A. Marathon in 2000, crossing the finish line hand-in-hand with, at the time, my eight-year-old daughter and my nine-year-old son in a very back-of-the-pack time of 8:45:54.*

For the next nine years, I thought many times about attempting to run a marathon again, but I stoically accepted my fate as a washed-up marathon has-been at the ripe old age of 37.

As the real estate market started to collapse in 2008, I experienced a series of financial setbacks, including the collapse of my own real estate investment house of cards, leaving my family in financial ruins. I subsequently fell into a pretty severe state of depression, and as a form of self-therapy, I returned to my running roots and became a daily recreational runner once again after many years of occasionally showing up, untrained, at local 5K or 10K races.

In March of 2009, I toed the line for the Pasadena Marathon. This time I had trained smart. I completed the marathon with a respectable sub-4 finish time—with no knee pain. About a month later, I ran a marathon on the Camp Pendleton U.S. Marine base, and a few weeks after that, I ran in a small race that was a 1.8-mile loop around a park and neighborhood. There were nine participants in the marathon that day. Simultaneously, there was a 3-, 6-, and 12-hour race taking place on the same course.

DC: Were you already looking past the marathon distance?

EE: *It was at that small loop marathon that I saw a white oval window decal on the back of an older model Volvo station wagon that simply read, "Badwater 135." Since this was such a small race, I made it my mission to hunt down this Badwater man or woman—I figured maybe women were running Badwater, too—and seek their advice on trying my hand at one of those really long 50K ultramarathons, but for some later time, way, way, way down the road. By golly, I was still wet behind the ears as a marathoner, only having recently completed two marathons in the previous two months, so I was still a long way off from being ready for one of those crazy far ultramarathon races.*

And regarding that completely ridiculous Badwater race, I had absolutely zero interest in ever entering that absurd race—a death-wish, 135-mile death march through Death Valley in the middle of July? In my mind, those people were simply out of their minds and should be locked up and the key thrown far, far away.

DC: Your ramp up to ultramarathons came when that Badwater competitor talked you into a 24-hour race. Who was that?

EE: *Yes, that was Steve Teal. When I finally tracked him down, he convinced me to sign up for the Nanny Goat 24-hour race, taking place in just two weeks, and assured me that there was no way I could DNF, as once I completed a single one-mile loop, a race finish was in the books, and it was all gravy from there. So that became my introduction to the ultramarathon. Not knowing any better, I skipped right over the 50K, 50-mile, 100K, and even the 100-mile, and ended up with 102 miles in 24-hours for my first ultramarathon experience. As they say, ignorance is bliss.*

RUNNING TO EXTREMES

DC: How could you go from having run only a couple marathons since 1980, to wearing a walking boot to get you through a marathon, to running 135 marathons in a year?

EE: *Just the same way everyone else completes every race they've ever entered. One step at a time, my friend, one step at a time. By the way, the "walking boot stories" seem to have taken on a life of their own, so maybe I should set the record straight on those.*

My daughter and son wanted to do the 2010 L.A. Marathon with me, 10 years after our first one, but my son was dealing with an injury, so I registered my daughter and me for the race. As fate would have it, a month before the race, I was diagnosed with a severe tibia stress fracture. I was given a walking boot, and since we had already paid for the race, I decided to see what I could do while wearing that darn boot. I told my daughter that I may not finish, but if I did, it would likely take over six hours. Long story short, we did finish the race hand-in-hand as we had 10 years earlier—just under six hours.

I did end up doing somewhere around 10 more marathons in the boot in the spring of 2010, including, one month later, the Boston to Big Sur marathon combo. One month after that, Nanny Goat number 2 was on the schedule. I figured that if I could complete all those marathons in a boot, why not a 24-hour race? I ended up with 102 miles, walking every step in the boot. I'm not sure if my current walking speed is up to 102 miles in 24-hours now—even if you paid me—but all those miles in the boot made for a strong walking ability. That strong power walk has since seen me safely through many, many 100-mile races.

By the way, I walked so many miles in that first walking boot that the heel wore right through to the sock, so I had to go back and get a second one from the doctor's office. That was an interesting conversation.

Two months after Nanny Goat, in July 2010, I crewed at Badwater 135 for Brian Recore, who I met for the first time at Nanny Goat. Brian had seen me in the boot, and although he was impressed with my boot-addled performance, he was rightly concerned as to whether or not I'd be able to properly crew and pace for him at Badwater. So at Badwater 2010, on Brian's crew, I was finally able to kick the boot to the curb and run boot free for the first time since February.

One week after Badwater 2010, I began my year-long marathon world record quest, ending 365 days later at Badwater 135 in July 2011 as my 135th marathon or ultra race in 365 days.

DC: Your first world record is running the most marathons in a year—135—and it has since been eclipsed. What did you get out of that experience?

EE: *A lot of things:*

- *I learned that if you set your mind to accomplishing a big goal, even if you don't quite reach it, the resulting journey is well worth the effort.*
- *I learned that if you shoot for the stars, you may not get there, but you might just land on the moon, and that's still a lofty accomplishment.*
- *I learned that just because something's never been done before, doesn't make it impossible. Improbable—maybe. Impossible—not necessarily.*
- *I learned that there are those who will support you, and those who will not. I chose to hang around those who supported me and ignore those who did not.*
- *I learned that many goals are best accomplished one step at a time, like simply focusing on just one race at a time, one aid station at a time, one hour at a time, one mile at a time, and, in some of those*

really dark times of a race, simply one step at a time, as sometimes the big picture was just too overwhelming.
- *I found that the human body is capable of accomplishing extraordinary things, if I listened to it, and heeded the message it was trying to tell me.*
- *I made a ton of new friends.*
- *I had so many priceless experiences that will provide joy to me until the day I die.*
- *I learned that my number one supporters were there from the beginning, not just in the celebratory final race, and those are the ones who really matter most—my closest friends, immediate family, and especially my amazing wife of 33 years, Saint Martha.*

DC: About your world record of finishing 40 100-mile or longer races in a year, how did you decide which races to run?

EE: The choice of which races to run typically came down to two specific criteria: logistics and cost. I would choose races that were in the same state, or a border state, or one or two states away. If I could drive to it, it was likely I would enter it. Now if I had to fly, that changed everything, due to the additional very costly travel expenses. And then there were the entry fees. I was quite blessed in that many race directors were supportive of what I was trying to accomplish, and knowing that I was, for the most part, unsponsored, they would help me with the entry fees, with discounts, or even comped entries. Many, certainly not all though. I still feel that if I had been blessed with sponsorship, many of those far away races that I had to pass up could have been on the agenda, and instead of a mere 40 100-mile races in one year, it could have certainly been 50, and maybe even closer to 60. The right person, a person with some extra money burning a hole in their pocket, or with a committed sponsor, will eventually lay waste to my silly little 40. But, it was the best my meager pocketbook could support at the time.

DC: Dean Karnazes ran 50 marathons in 50 days, and he said the toughest part was the logistics. Did you have similar issues to overcome, like actually finding enough races in a year?

EE: *Well, Dean and I traveled two different paths. He completed a marathon in all 50 states in 50 days. A large number of his marathons, although on legitimate marathon courses, were run on days that best fit his very tight schedule. So although they were on established marathon courses, they weren't actual marathon races. But I don't begrudge him that—his quest, his rules.*

I highly respect Dean and each of his amazing accomplishments. The subsequent exposure and goodwill that he's brought to our sport is unmatched. I'm proud to say that he had a positive influence on my ultra aspirations when I was just starting out as well, from reading his best seller, Ultramarathon Man. Some of his stories—like the portrayal of his Badwater expeditions—were a bit shocking, but that didn't dissuade me from eventually venturing into that race and various other difficult ultras. And on the few occasions that I've had the good fortune to see him at a race, he's always been a good sport and a true gentleman.

So, not to take anything away from Dean's 50/50 accomplishments, but we were attempting two completely different quests, so it's kind of like comparing apples to oranges. Although we both had major logistical challenges to overcome, they were unique to our quests. Dean had to squeeze in 50 marathons in 50 days, and each of the 50 had to be in a different state. I had to try to complete 40 (my goal from the beginning), but I could choose any combination of 40 from over 100 options for 100-mile races throughout the United States, or actually anywhere around the world if I chose to go beyond our bounders. So Dean was much more limited in his options than I was. One thing I did choose to do differently, I committed from the start to only doing official races. Now, where I

RUNNING TO EXTREMES

differed from Liz Bauer's quest (current women's record holder, with 36 100-mile races in 2012) and Scott Brockmeier's quest (former male record holder, with 27 100-mile races in 2012) is that I chose any race that had a 100-mile or longer option, including fixed-time races such as 24-hour and multi-day races, whereas Liz and Scott chose to stick with strictly 100-mile races, specifically. So they chose to follow a different set of guidelines. Their quest, their rules.

By entering races such as Badwater 135, Nanny Goat 24-Hour, Silverton 72-Hour, Across the Years 144-Hour, I had more options to choose from. With that said, I always counted any official race that was at least 100 miles or more and only counted each race as one race toward the record. For example, I participated in a six-day race in Anchorage in which I completed 415 miles, but I counted that as a single 100-mile race toward the total, not four separate 100s. In the end, I had enough "bonus" miles with my forty 100-plus-mile races that my total race distance for those 40 races wasn't 4,000 miles on the nose, but instead totaled 4,802 miles. As we're fond of saying in ultras, "bonus miles are always free."

DC: Perhaps the most impressive feat of all was when you did two 100-mile races in a weekend—twice!

EE: *Yes, one of my biggest challenges was completing two 100-mile races in the same weekend (well, Friday to Sunday), in two different states: Utah and California. [Most Utah 100s typically start on a Friday.] I did not want any special favors or rule exemptions from the RDs, so I committed from the start to make all the same time cutoffs as everyone else in the race.*

On that first attempt of back-to-back races, I started race number one at 5:00 a.m. on a Friday in Utah, finished in 21:45, and was on a flight from Salt Lake City, heading to LAX, by 6:00 a.m. on Saturday. I arrived at the second race over an hour after the 7:00 a.m. start, which meant I was up against the clock for making checkpoints at 25 miles and 50 miles, but scraped through those by the skin of my teeth, finishing race number two on Sunday around noon with nearly an hour to spare. I definitely was burning the candle at both ends on that three-day weekend.

In my second attempt at completing two back-to-back 100-mile races in one weekend, I was going for the big one: my record tying number 36 and record-breaking number 37. I stayed awake pretty much nonstop for those two races, from Friday morning at 6 a.m. doing the first race—102 miles in 23:50—and then starting the second race at 6 a.m. on Saturday, with a 10-minute break between the two. The second 100 took me just under 36 hours. At points I was literally sleepwalking, with friends walking along on both sides of me, keeping me from veering off course.

One of my biggest physical challenges for the year was trying to overcome all the various little niggles that showed up without warning that could easily have turned into serious injuries if not addressed swiftly. Luckily, I was able to nip them in the bud early on. Being married to a very experienced licensed massage therapist helped tremendously. I refer to her abilities as my secret weapon. By keeping my body from falling apart, my biggest streak was a run of 13 100- mile race weekends in a row, ending with Badwater 135 on lucky weekend number 13.

One of the rare occasions in which I didn't give my wife a chance to use her magic touch was at Badwater. I strained my TFL [one of the hip abductor muscles] early on in the race, and instead of giving her a chance to work on it, I tried muscling through it, afraid that I might not make the time cutoffs. I ended up limping through the last 85 of the 135 miles, reduced to a walk. Less than two weeks after Badwater was my six-day race in Alaska. With enough time for my wife to work her magic, I was able to show up at the race healthy and strong and completed 415 miles over the six days.

DC: Similar to my question about your marathons, what did you get out of your 100-miler feat?

EE: *Everything that I got out of the marathon world record, I got out of the 100-mile world record, tenfold. I had so much more support this time around, maybe because I knew so many more runners in 2014 compared to 2010-2011. Also, having completed one world record, it gives you a lot of confidence when attempting another one. I got so much more satisfaction out of the process, being able to enjoy every race for its own merits and share the race experience with so many more people as we spent quality time together on the course.*

When you're running marathons, and each one takes an average of four hours, it's a race, and the focus is on finishing as fast as you can. But there's no doubt in your mind that you will certainly finish the 26.2 miles. But when you're migrating through a 100-mile race that could take anywhere from 20 to 36 hours, it's a journey of trials and tribulations mutually shared by all those around you. And every single time you toe the line at a 100-mile race, you realize that this may be the one you don't finish, since the drop rate at most 100-mile races is typically 20 to 40 percent, sometimes more. One race I entered in Texas had an 80 percent drop rate due to the course conditions exacerbated by stormy weather, and I was the very last finisher, beating the hard (read, strict) cutoff by mere seconds. I also had the joy of rediscovering at every race that the human body and mind are capable of so much more than we can imagine if we can just let our imaginations run free, uninhibited by societal norms.

DC: What's the backstory on your jester moniker and your wild hat and outfit?

EE: *The jester persona came about quite by accident. I was a founding member and board president of a new marathon training club named Riverside Road Runners. Our main purpose was to turn beginner walkers and runners into marathon athletes in seven months, using the Galloway Run Walk Run training program. Our targeted marathon was the Surf City Marathon in Huntington Beach. As a lark, the club secretary, Ramona Fiero, and I presented a little skit, "Surfer Dude Asks Professor Moe." As Surfer Dude, I was dressed in some crazy, loud board shorts, a Hawaiian print shirt, flip-flops, and a visor with spiked blond hair. I'm totally bald, so that by itself was a big hit. The skit went well and garnered some laughs, so I decided it would be fun to show up at the upcoming Surf City Marathon as my alter ego, Surfer Dude.*

This seemed to enhance the marathon experience of not only our club members, but also others in the race, as well, especially near the finish line where I waited and cheered until the last walker completed their 26.2-mile odyssey. My goal was to remind all of us, including myself, not to take ourselves too seriously. This was in 2010 or 2011. Shortly after that, I started wearing the most outrageous, colorful board shorts I could get my hands on, and living in SoCal, that wasn't too difficult, and I begin wearing various silly hats I would purchase for a couple bucks at Goodwill stores. At one point, I put a jester hat on my head, and it just seemed to be the right fit, literally as well as figuratively. From that point on, my bald head was adorned with a jester hat, and then my wife put her magical fingers to work, designing and sewing a colorful jester skirt, complete with jester bells. After Badwater, I started wearing white tights in all my races. My friend, Teresa, from Ultra Gam Gaiters made me some custom arm sleeves, gaiters, and neck wraps, and the rest, as they say, is history.

DC: Eric Clifton also considers himself a jester, and is included in this book. Is this a trend?

EE: *I sure hope so. Wouldn't that be a hoot! A bunch a mini-jesters running around helping other runners at races.*

When I first became the Jester, I had no idea that someone with such admirable stature in the ultra community was the original jester—Eric Clifton. Since then, I've gotten to know Eric quite well and was blown away when I learned of his long-running records and various running exploits. I hope he feels that I'm doing justice to those high jester antics—I mean standards—that he initially set forth.

Maybe someday, someone new will come along to continue on with this honored jester tradition and take over as the new jester, but hopefully not any time too soon, as I feel I have a few good running years left in these jester bones. By the way, Eric lives a mere 10 miles from me. We cross paths from time to time when we're out and about, but mostly I see him at local training runs and races.

DC: What's left to do for Ed Ettinghausen, the Jester?

EE: *Bucket list races still on the horizon? Spartathlon, Comrades, New York City Marathon, Marine Corp Marathon, Chicago Marathon, Hardrock 100, Barkley Marathons, and Western States 100. I keep waiting for my lucky lottery number to be drawn for Western States 100. The way the lottery is conducted, my odds increase exponentially each year, so I just need to bide my time.*

The way I look at it, it's like the guy or gal who tries to get a Boston qualifying time, year after year. When they finally get in, they appreciate the Boston Marathon experience that much more. When I do finally get into States, I'll probably be the only person in the history of the race to run their maiden voyage of Western States with the experience of over one hundred 100s under their belt. We'll see if that gives me any advantage.

I would also like to take a shot at the USA Transcontinental record, unbeaten since 1982, of 46 days and 8 hours. I think I could give that record a run for the money. And just for the jester fun of it, I'd like to get a large group of friends together to try to break the Guinness World Record for the largest marathon centipede. That could be a lot of fun. Plus, I've got my eye on some additional American and world records (besides the four I currently hold) — age division and open records — that I'd still like to target. Really, I could run until I'm 100 and still not run out of fun races, or crazy race goals, or fun ways to run races with my friends.

CHAPTER 15

ANN TRASON

I consider it a great honor to write the introduction for Ann Trason. I will not go into her incredible running accomplishments, for these will be addressed in the following chapter. Instead, I will focus on my personal experiences with Ann. I have been a participant in sports for almost 70 years. I have also been able to see some of the great performances by the world's greatest athletes. I've seen Jim Brown play football, Willie Mays play baseball, Wayne Gretzky play hockey, Michael Jordan play basketball, and, most importantly, Ann Trason, the greatest ultramarathon runner in history. You may have noticed I did not say the greatest female ultramarathon runner, but rather the greatest ultramarathon runner. When Ann competed, she simply was the best.

I will only speak of Ann's accomplishments at Western States Endurance Run, long considered to be the Super Bowl of 100-mile mountain trail races and also the race my wife, Helen, and I directed for 14 years, from 1986 to 1999. Against perhaps the finest group of 100-mile trail runners this country had to offer, Ann not only won the women's division 14 times, but she also finished second and third overall two times each against a star-studded field.

On occasion, Ann could appear a bit aloof and a bit temperamental. The pressure she put on herself to perform and to try to stay focused could, at times, become very difficult when just prior to a big event people wanted to interview her, photograph her, or asked her for an autograph. These distractions could certainly add to this pressure and her ability to remain focused. Adding to the pressure, occasionally Ann suffered stomach problems during the race (feelings of nausea and the complications accompanying it). Fortunately she learned how to deal with these problems while continuing to run. Her discipline during these episodes was truly remarkable.

RUNNING TO **EXTREMES**

One story I always like to tell about Ann occurred in 1990. Helen and I were in Portland, Oregon, where Helen was competing in Megan's 24-Hour Track Run. On Sunday morning following the race, we went back to our hotel and turned on the television. Live coverage of the Portland Marathon was on the screen, and the announcers were continually talking about two local women runners who were battling it out for the lead. They went to a commercial break, and when they came back on, they were more than surprised when a woman they had never heard of had taken over the lead. It so happens that Ann, who was visiting friends in Portland, had entered the marathon on a lark at the last minute. She went on to win in 2:43. I talked to Ann on several occasions after that and encouraged her to focus on marathon training and forget the 100-mile trail runs for a while because I felt confident she could have qualified for the U.S. Olympic marathon team. But she wasn't interested. She may not have beaten the Kenyans or the Ethiopians, but her presence would certainly have been felt.

Today, there are many great female ultramarathon runners, and there will be many more great ones to come, but rest assured there will never be another Ann Trason. Helen and I feel very fortunate to have seen her complete and have had her participate in races that we directed. We also feel very honored having her as our friend.

–Norm Klein

TRAIL BLAZER

By Scott Ludwig

Like most runners, Ann Trason wears a chronograph when she runs. But unlike most runners, she's not using it to time her runs; rather it's to set the alarm to remind her to eat every 30 minutes. After all, it's important that anyone running 10-minute miles up and down mountainous terrain for 17 hours or so replace the 10,000 calories they'll burn in the process.

Just ask Ann, who has won the prestigious 100-mile Western States Endurance Run an unprecedented—and highly unlikely to be duplicated—14 times. Former Western States race director, Norm Klein, calls her "not only the best female ultrarunner of all time, but *the* best ultrarunner of all time." A quick glance at her résumé in the sport makes it difficult to argue with him.

Here are just a few of the highlights of Ann Trason's amazing career:

> The aforementioned 14 Western States championships between 1989 and 2003, including a women's division course record of 17:37:51 (1994) that wasn't broken for 18 years (Ellie Greenwood, 2012).
>
> The women's course record at the Leadville Trail 100-Mile Run (18:06:24 in 1994) and an overall finish of second place.
>
> Two-time winner of the Comrades Marathon (1996 and 1997, and both times winning Western States a mere 12 days later).

RUNNING TO EXTREMES

> Course records at many other ultramarathons, including the Miwok 100K Trail Race, the Wasatch Front 100-Mile Endurance Run, and the American River 50-Mile Endurance Run.

In a sport measured by hours, minutes, and seconds, it's unlikely to find a runner the caliber of Ann Trason who isn't a slave to the clock (other than her aforementioned half-hour need to replace calories while running long-distance events).

The explanation is quite simple, actually: Ann Trason enjoys living in the moment. One moment, in particular, at Western States provides all the support that is needed for validation.

Ann was running toward the Rucky Chucky River crossing (approximately mile 88) along a long, rocky stretch of jeep road when she tripped over an impediment *(Rock? Stick?)* and fell to the ground. Those around her questioned why a veteran Western States runner of her talent and experience would fall at arguably the easiest section of the course to run. Her answer was short, precise. and to the point: "I was looking at the view."

The Sierra Nevada Mountains are one of Ann's favorite places to run. The first time she was introduced to the magnificence, the beauty, and the danger of the rugged foliage and terrain, she knew she was where she wanted to be. How she got there is a story worthy of legend. But first it's important to know how it all began.

Ann's father, Czechoslovakian by birth, and her mother, a Canadian, were both educators. For the record, the Czechoslovakian spelling of Ann's last name is Trasonova. Ann also has a brother and believes the two of them were fortunate to have such supportive parents as they were growing up.

Ann started running in junior high school (in the days before Title IX when the athletic world offered little opportunity for women to excel). Her dad provided her all the encouragement and confidence she needed, and it wasn't long before she was excelling at a sport suited for daddy's little girl who always seemed to have so much energy, as Ann so fondly recalls. It wasn't long before she joined a track-and-field team and did so well she was offered an athletic scholarship to run at the University of New Mexico. Unfortunately, she was never able to run at the collegiate level due to injuries, so she turned her attention to getting an education. She transferred to UC Berkeley and graduated with honors in Nutrition Science.

After graduating from college, the young woman with so much energy became—as one might expect—bored. Ann competed in a half Ironman, and, although she finished, she nearly drowned in the swimming and had problems with the cycling. She had no problem with the running and realized that's really what she wanted to do and, more importantly, what she was *meant* to do.

Ann idolized a young woman named Sally Edwards (now in the Triathlete Hall of Fame) who had the course record at the aforementioned half Ironman. So when Ann ran her first 50-miler at American River in 1985 (at first she thought the race flyer had an extra zero after the five, but when she stood corrected, she still decided to run the race, even though she had never run anything farther than a 10K), and midway through the race, she found herself running side by side with her idol.

"Oh my god, it's Sally Edwards," she thought to herself. Sally looked to Ann, sighed, and asked her if she were a rabbit (someone running a specific pace for a portion of a race to help another runner maintain their pace). That was all that was needed to light the competitive spark in Ann

RUNNING TO EXTREMES

Trason. As Ann describes it: "She hurt my feelings, so I took off." Ann, then 24 years old and running in her very first ultramarathon, not only won the race, but also established a new course record as well. "I had a good day," she said in reflection. Even though the temperature reached 108 degrees Fahrenheit, and she didn't know carrying water as she ran was highly recommended (if not essential), she still "had a good day." It was pretty obvious Ann had discovered her niche.

Ann would have another good day at the same race eight years later when she lowered her course record by an hour to 6:09:08. (Ann could not remember her exact finishing time, but she thought it was around 7:30, "not really a great time," she said. Ann's limited recollection of her accomplishments is one of the things making her the charismatic person that she is. You're about to read another.)

While Ann doesn't remember the time of her first victory and first course record, she does remember seeing a little boy sitting at the finish line with the saddest look on his face. She went up to him and asked what was wrong. The little boy said he was waiting for his dad to finish, so Ann asked him if he enjoyed his dad racing. "No!" he said. Ann asked why. "Because his socks always stink after he does one of these!" These are the stories Ann remembers and enjoys telling. For her, running is not about the times, the distances, the victories, or the course records; it's about the people and the experiences.

Then Ann heard about someone running 100 miles, a challenge she thought was psychotic. Six months later, a friend invited her to run the first 30 miles of the course that hosted the Western States Endurance Run, the premier 100-mile race in the country. She instantly fell in love with the trail and right then and there decided she was going to dedicate her life to it. She fell, she got dirty, she lost her way a few times, but none of that mattered. Ann remembers it as the moment that transformed her life. "It's California, it's the mountains, it's high, and it's my friend," she said. It wouldn't be long before Ann Trason would make her mark in the world of ultrarunning on these very trails.

About six months after calling 100-miles psychotic, Ann found herself at the starting line of the Western States Endurance Run in Squaw Valley, California. The year was 1987. If you're not familiar with the first four miles of the race, the trail runs straight up the side of a mountain. Straight. Up. The. Side. Of. A. Mountain. Ann was not intimidated, however, as she ran up that very same mountain as a teenager when she was in Squaw Valley while it was being used as a training camp for the Winter Olympic team. But that first time running to the top of Squaw Valley gave her a dose of reality, if only for a moment. "Oh my god, I thought I was going to die," she said.

But this time, after making it to the top, there would be 96 more miles remaining before reaching the finish line in Auburn. It didn't end well, as Ann dropped out due to problems with her knee and just generally being what she called stupid. She returned a year later, and the results were the same: another DNF (did not finish), although she made it to the Highway 49 checkpoint (just over 93 miles into the race) only to have a doctor at the aid station slap an IV on her to replenish her dehydrated body, signaling the end of the race for her. Reflecting back, she said she could have walked to reach the finish line and could possibly have avoided the race-ending encounter with the doctor.

Ann was really depressed after failing for the second time. She spent a week in her parent's cabin on their property near the trail to figure out all the things she did wrong because she really still wanted to run Western States. Then the problem solving began: How could I have done this differently? Ann's short list of solutions: Remember to drink, replace electrolytes throughout the race, pace myself, and don't panic.

RUNNING TO **EXTREMES**

Ann admits she learned more in those first two years than she did in a lifetime. She's gone on to use those solutions in her running and her coaching ever since.

Had she not spent that week addressing those problems, the next 15 years of the history of ultrarunning might have been dramatically different, because during that span, Ann Trason would win all 14 of the Western States Endurance Runs she entered. (Note: Ann competed every year between 1989 and 2003 with the exception of 1999.) Ann returned to Squaw Valley in 1989 at the bequest of then race director, Norm Klein, a man who she obviously holds near and dear to her heart. "The race wouldn't be what it is today without him. He really got people to consider to volunteer; it's not just all about running," Anne says.

Following is a complete list of Ann's Western States finishes, every one of them women's division championships.

1989	18:47:46	10th place overall (at the age of 28)
1990	18:33:02	10th place overall
1991	18:29:37	9th place overall
1992	18:14:18	3rd place overall
1993	19:05:22	3rd place overall
1994	17:37:51	2nd place overall (women's course record)
1995	18:40:01	2nd place overall (less than five minutes behind overall champion)

1996	18:57:36	3rd place overall
1997	19:19:49	8th place overall
1998	18:46:16	4th place overall
1999		Did not compete
2000	19:44:42	11th place overall
2001	18:33:34	6th place overall
2002	18:16:26	6th place overall
2003	18:36:03	8th place overall (at the age of 42)

When asked about her most memorable Western States, Ann didn't mention her first victory, her women's course record, or her finish less than a mile behind the winner in 1995. It was her ninth-place finish in 1991—a cold year, according to Ann. Ann admittedly doesn't do well in the cold. Ann was perfectly content with her position when told by a volunteer along the course she was in 24th or 25th place. But her pacer, Gary Neel, had other ideas. "Now you have your work cut out for you," she remembers him saying. "You can still finish in the top ten." When they reached Highway 49, a volunteer told them they were in 10th place. According to Ann, she ran the last six miles with a big fork in her back, which is what she says as she vividly remembers the experience of running with her friend who passed away much too young. Gary, who never smoked a day in his life, was later diagnosed with lung cancer and succumbed to the terrible disease in 2007, at 51 years of age.

RUNNING TO EXTREMES

It's apparent by this recollection that memories are more important to Ann than victories. Her responses to a series of rapid-fire questions provide all the support that is needed.

Q: What is your 100-mile personal best?

A: I think it is 13 hours and something. [Actually 13:47:42 on the road in 1990. Ann's 100-mile best on the track is 14:29:44 in 1989.]

Q: Your 50-mile personal best?

A: Five hours and something. [Actually 5:40:18 in 1991.]

Q: 24-hour best?

A: I remember that! It was at Flushing Meadows [New York], and it was pouring rain, and Ted Corbitt came out! It may have been the hardest thing I ever did because of the conditions: crazy, crazy rain. But it was such an honor and a pleasure to meet Ted Corbitt. I couldn't believe he came out to watch us run. [Ann never mentioned that she ran more than 143 miles in the event.]

Q: How many miles have you run in your lifetime?

A: I would not know. I haven't a clue.

Q: How many races have you run?

A: I have no clue.

Q: How many 100-milers have you run?

A: Somewhere in the 20s, maybe. Not sure.

Q: How many races have you won?

A: Dunno. [A viable source of ultramarathon performances on the Internet reports that between 1985 and 2004, Ann won 49 of the 51 events she finished. Apparently the thought of mentioning this never crossed her mind.]

What stands out is Ann remembered meeting one of her idols at a 24-hour endurance run in 1989. The fact she ran more than 143 miles there and couldn't immediately answer the other rapid-fire questions posed to her says all you need to know about what Ann Trason considers important.

Ann mentioned at one time she kept a running log and was running 200 miles a week. Today she would give anything to run 100 miles a week. It's possible the wear and tear from so many years of world-class running has taken a toll on her body. That may be the case, but if so, it certainly hasn't dampened her spirit.

Ann took a 10-year hiatus from running between 2004 and 2013. Ann explains why: "The person I was with at the time couldn't run and bicycling was a way to spend time together." During that time she did a lot of ultracycling and rode across the country for her 50th birthday. She enjoyed getting out of her comfort zone (she doesn't consider herself a great cyclist) and spending time with the person she cared about. It wasn't until early 2013 that Ann returned to her comfort zone: running.

While she no longer considers herself competitive, she now enjoys pacing and crewing for other runners, thus giving back to the sport she so dearly loves. Ann says she's had more rewarding experiences in the last couple of years since she turned her attention toward helping others.

RUNNING TO **EXTREMES**

Ann's rewarding experiences began in earnest back in 2000 when she took over the directorship of the Dick Collins Firetrails 50 after the founder and namesake of the race—who was a mentor of Ann's—passed away. Ann loved the race that had been around since 1983 and didn't want to see it end. She would go on to be the race director for 11 years before passing the torch to someone else. During those 11 years, Ann didn't make any money for her efforts, a testament to how much she believes in giving back to the sport. It's interesting to note that the number of runners in the Firetrails 50 more than tripled in the 10 years of Ann's tenure as race director.

Another of Ann's mentors is Dan Williams, a 21-time finisher of Western States. At one time, Ann babysat Dan's daughter, Christina, and took her for a run when she was 11 years old. Ann gave her a pair of Nike running shoes and either a Western States medal or T-shirt (she couldn't remember for sure) and with the familial ties to the race, it was only a matter of time before Christina had a vision of running Western States. Her vision would later become reality. Let the record reflect that Christina Williams, age 29, finished the 2013 Western States Endurance Run. Her former babysitter was by her side, pacing her for the final 38 miles. They crossed the finish line together; the clock read 27:01:51, a terrific performance for a Western States rookie.

Ann has a certain fondness for sixth graders, approximately the age when Christina Williams ran with her for the first time. Ann fondly remembers something an 11-year-old girl said to her recently: "You're not like the person in *Born to Run*. You're more fun!" (Note: It's apparent Ann wasn't happy with the way she was portrayed in the book, although she has too much class to comment on it for this story. The book describes her as an aggressive competitor. In reality, she is nothing but humble and gracious.)

Ann candidly admits the enthusiasm of the students she is coaching is what drew her back into the sport she so dearly loves. She says, "Their joy of running is what showed me how much I missed it."

Ann is currently involved with launching her online coaching business. A casual viewing of her website indicates it's going to be a success. Here are comments from two of her students:

I found Ann to be not only very personable and down to earth, but she also had a way of inspiring and motivating me. As my coach, Ann helped me to realize that I'm capable of much more than I had imagined.

She challenged me to use introspection during training; it was during these moments of reflection that I took stock of the lessons I learned and also prepared myself for whatever scenarios might arise during the race. What Ann called the three Ps—planning, preparation, progress—worked together so well that on race day, I felt excited, confident, and unafraid of the leap I was going to make. It turned out to be the most amazing race of my life.

To say that anyone would feel privileged to have Ann Trason as a personal coach is an understatement. However, for Ann, it also presents a catch-22 situation: She has given coaching advice to fellow runners all of her life, and to charge money for these same services goes against her inherent desire to give back. But as everyone knows, people have to earn a living, and what better way to earn a living than doing something that you truly enjoy?

Today Ann continues to run. She enjoys the freedom it offers. She enjoys helping people. She enjoys the space it offers from life's daily challenges.

RUNNING TO EXTREMES

Most of all—and make no mistake about it—Ann simply enjoys running. It may be nice that she broke 20 world records in distances up to 100 miles; qualified three times for the U.S. Olympic marathon trials; won Western States 14 times; and set a course record at the Leadville 100 that has held up for more than two decades. Yes, all of those accomplishments are indeed nice.

Nice, but not nearly as important as the simple act of running for the sake of running. She's content knowing she no longer has the legs up to the challenge of running the times she was capable of in her prime. Rather, she's grateful she continues to be able to run and be a viable part of the sport that has given her so much joy and satisfaction since she was just a little girl.

Ann lives in the San Francisco Bay area and enjoys running in the neighboring mountains, sometimes venturing as far away as Mount Tamalpais in Marin County (a 20-minute drive from her home to the trailhead, but well worth it!). The tile in her house is made from the red clay from these very mountains; she believes the red clay is truly magic.

Truly magic. The same can be said about Ann Trason.

Author's note: During the ongoing telephone and email conversations I conducted with Ann Trason during the course of writing her story, I sent her a photograph of my six-year-old grandson's legs after he ran his first trail race. It was raining during the race, and by the time he reached the finish, his legs were both covered in mud. My note to her read:

Hi Ann. My grandson ran his first one-mile trail race Saturday.

I thought you'd get a kick out of seeing his legs.

Ann wrote back:

Awesome picture! I do hope you visit here. Come out for Western States!

Your write up made my friend and I [sic!] *laugh. Thanks. Ann.*

No, Ann. Thank *YOU!*

AUTHORS AND CONTRIBUTORS

This book would be incomplete if its authors and contributors were not formally acknowledged. In fact, if you wanted to write a sequel, you could choose your subject matter from the following list of people, all *extreme* in their own way.

Presented in alphabetical order, any one of them is apt to be found in various lists of who's who in the world of running.

Steve Boone—Steve lives and runs in Humble, Texas. He has over 600 marathon finishes to his credit that include a marathon in all 50 states five times and more than 200 in the state of Texas. He co-founded the 50 States Marathon Club with his wife, Paula, in 2001, which now boasts a membership of 3,700. He started and continues to fund the Marathon Challenge Program, which awards T-shirts to local elementary school children who complete the marathon distance during the academic school year. Over the last 22 years, the program has grown from 14 finishers the first year to 9,300 finishers in 2014. Steve and Paula traveled to Kochi, India, in 2014 to start the program in their local elementary schools.

Bonnie Busch—Born, raised, and still living in Iowa, Bonnie has been doing information technology work for over 25 years for an equipment manufacturer. She started recreational running in 1982 in order to complete the Bix 7-Mile Road Race with a group of friends. She accidentally discovered ultrarunning six years later through a local 24-hour run and slowly started to discover ultrarunning events from 50K to multi-day adventures on both roads and trails. Among her credentials are 40-plus races of 100 miles or more, 200-plus ultramarathon finishes, the 1995 National USA 24-Hour Female Championship, four Badwater finishes, a solo run across Iowa, and learning how to swim in 2005 and going on to complete 15 Ironman races. Bonnie is still running and willing to try just about anything once.

Gary Corbitt—Gary is retired from a 38-year career in Media Research. Today, he focuses his attention on preserving the history of long-distance running. As curator of the Ted Corbitt Archives, his primary mission is preserving his father's legacy and that of the other founding fathers of long-distance running.

Gary has had a unique view of watching the sport being invented. He considers himself a historian of the sport and remembers when women couldn't officially run in road races or race in track meets farther than 800 meters. As a child and teenager, Gary often volunteered in various capacities at races. He has been a fan of the sport since the early 1960s and continues to run races today in the 60 to 64 age category.

David Corfman—David began running marathons in 1997, and four years later he began adding ultramarathons to his résumé. Today, he has over 60 finishes in both. His running accomplishments include a silver buckle at Western States in 2009, a Badwater finish in 2010, and 1,000-mile buckles at both the Mohican 100-Mile Trail Race and the Potawatomi Trail Race. He currently leads pace groups at marathons and directs the Stone Steps 50K Trail Race in Cincinnati while continuing to race long distances. David's favorite race distance is 100 miles, where he has painfully learned that no finish is ever given or assumed, and every finish is a triumph.

Dave Dial—Dave grew up in rural east Texas and had a horse before he ever had a bicycle. However, he is fond of saying he found his legs first. With that in mind, it was as a child he initially discovered his love for running. By his teen years, having already run numerous miles on dirt roads and through forest trails in the Davy Crockett National Forest—to get from one place to another or simply for fun—he began keeping a running log in a spiral notebook. Some 40-odd years later, Dave, currently working as a cattle ranch foreman on land owned by his family for decades, has amassed over 176,000 lifetime miles. He also serves as an ambassador for Injinji Footwear in addition to wear-testing high-performance athletic shoes for Sketchers.

Mark Falcone—Mark is retired after 30 years working in the field of technology. He met Tim Twietmeyer 15 years ago when the two of them stopped working for Corporate America and ventured into their own start-up. Mark and Tim run, ride, and serve as long-term board members of the Western States Endurance Run Foundation. They both share a love for the preservation of trails.

David Horton—David is a professor of Exercise Science at Liberty University in Lynchburg, Virginia. He currently directs three ultramarathons: Holiday Lake 50K, Promise Land 50K, and Hellgate 100K. David ran for 33 years, compiling over 113,000 miles and 160 ultramarathons. He set speed records for the 2,144-mile Appalachian Trail in 1991 and the 2,650-mile Pacific Crest Trail in 2005. After injuring his knee in 2010 (requiring a total knee replacement in 2014), David converted to ultra-distance mountain biking and has completed the 2,700-mile Tour Divide (2011) and has plans to do it again in the near future.

Ben Jones—Ben, a three-time finisher of the Badwater Ultramarathon, was inducted into the Badwater Hall of Fame in 2010. "The Mayor of Badwater" (as Ben is known) and his wife, Denise (the "First Lady," who was also inducted), were recognized for their years of service on the race course as athletes, camp hosts, volunteers, crew members, and race ambassadors. Denise has crewed for Ben three times at Badwater and has this to say about him: "He is delightful to crew, one of the best-natured people on the planet, never complains, and is always kind, and crewing was always fun."

Norm Klein—Norm and his wife, Helen, served as co-race directors for 100 races of marathon distance or longer, including the prestigious Western States Endurance Run for 14 years (1986–1999) and the Helen Klein ultra events for 16 years (1995–2010). An athlete himself, Norm completed over 40 marathons, 40 ultramarathons, an Ironman (Hawaii), and a 125-mile staged race in the Himalayas. In May 2016, Norm and Helen will celebrate their 49th wedding anniversary.

Scott Ludwig—Scott has dabbled in many of the "festivities" chronicled in this book. From a sixth-place finish in the 2003 Badwater Ultramarathon to a last-place finish in the 2006 Western States Endurance run (as well as a DNF in 2004), in his prime, he was game for most anything. With a running streak that began on November 30, 1978, he has his sights focused on the two dozen or more runners in front of him with longer streaks. Scott has also authored five other books about running and co-authored another. Switching gears a bit, he would like to one day find a second career writing human-interest stories and books—à la Lewis Grizzard—and enjoy being a G-Pa. Once he retires from his day job, of course.

Susan Paraska—Susan ran her first race (a 5K) on July 4, 1986, in Montgomery, Alabama. While living in Colorado in the 1990s, she began running 10Ks. After moving to Atlanta, Georgia, she discovered a robust and rich running community offering year-round running at every distance. She completed her first ultra in 2008 (Peachtree City 50K) and her first 100-mile run four years later at the Bartram 100 in Milledgeville, Georgia. Susan is an active member of the Galloway

RUNNING TO EXTREMES

Program and the Darkside Running Club. She is a retired military officer and a certified project manager currently living in Marietta, Georgia.

Chris Roman—Chris is 45 years young and is a doctor, husband, father, philanthropist, and ultrarunner (although not necessarily in that order). In 2004, he decided to get his health back and began training for a marathon that he would eventually complete in slightly less than four hours. Four years later, he ran his first 100-mile race in Leadville, Colorado. Since then he has completed some of the more challenging races on the planet, including Badwater (twice) and the Brazil 135 (four times). Chris also holds the American course record on both the 135-mile and 175-mile courses of the Brazil 135. At this time, he is the only person to have run the length of the Erie Canal (344 miles in a little over six days) and one of three people to successfully run Brazil's *Camniho da Fe* (Path of Faith), which he did in just over seven days (while completing the Brazil 135 along the way). Since 2008, Chris has finished 25 races of 100 miles or more. The best part, he says, is he has fun every step and now has two distinct families that care for him as much as he cares for them.

Erin Roman—Forever student, teacher, designer, mother, seeker, Erin's passions run deep. As a committed student and teacher of yoga, Erin has been a dedicated practitioner for over 10 years. Mother of two active daughters and wife to her very active husband, her family is her greatest joy and comfort. When she's not running carpool or keeping up with Chris' race schedule, she enjoys cooking vegetarian meals for her family, writing blogs, making jewelry, and chasing after their three rescue dogs. In 2014, she expanded her creative reach and opened Carma Blue, her small business "love child." A full plate of family, friends, lesson learning, and big belly laughs, her life is perfectly imperfect, and she wouldn't have it any other way.

Erik Schaffer—Erik, a fully certified prosthetist, opened the doors to his own facility, A Step Ahead Prosthetics, in Hicksville, New York, in 2001. His philosophy of exacting craftsmanship, innovation, and providing a wide variety of prosthetic services under one roof has successfully extended to his business, creating a full ecosystem of support for patients. Erik is considered to be one of the foremost authorities on prosthetic technology, and A Step Ahead is known as *the* destination for amputees looking for the ultimate in prosthetic care. Erik and his staff were responsible for providing prosthetic care to survivors of the 2013 Boston Marathon bombing.

Craig Snapp—Craig celebrated his 39th year as a runner in 2015 and during that time has never pushed himself to the limits of human endurance, although in recent times he's getting closer to his *own* limits. While not claiming to be an ultrarunner (with only seven runs longer than marathon distance, the longest being 50 miles), he does have a total of 144 marathons and ultramarathons to his credit. One of his memorable moments in running was as a spectator, watching a young Jim Ryun obliterate the high school mile record in 1965 (Ryun ran 3:55.3), which would not be bettered for another 36 years. Having run every single day since April 1, 1998, Craig has managed to accumulate well over 100,000 miles in his running career.

Jon Sutherland—Jon is the current record holder for the longest running streak in America as certified by the USRSA, over 45 years and counting. Jon said, "There is no way I would have ever considered a running streak without my teammate, Mark Covert, telling me he had run every day for a year. I made a year without missing a day and was fascinated by the journey it took to be a good runner." Jon is an accomplished rock journalist and writer who has been published in over 60 magazines worldwide and has written five books. His passion, though, has always been running. Jon competed at an international level and raced in many U.S. national championships. Currently, Jon is the cross-country coach at Notre Dame High School in Sherman Oaks, California, and enjoys running on the trails behind his house with his dogs, Puck and Pixie.

Heather Ulrich—Heather was lucky to be born to Rory and Janis Vose and to grow up in Winona, Minnesota, with her two sisters, Laura and Tahra. A bit of a tomboy, she went canoeing, camping, hunting, and fishing with her dad; enjoyed horseback riding and Girl Scouts; fell in love with the mountains when working in Yellowstone National Park; and moved permanently to Colorado in the spring of 1990. She met Marshall Ulrich at the Leadville Trail 100 Run in 2001 and happily married him April 1, 2003. (They chose that date because they joked, "People will think we're *fools* to be getting married.") While not a runner herself, she enjoys traveling and adventures with Marshall all around the world.

Andy Velazco—Andy started running over 30 years ago while serving in the U.S. Army during a hiatus between college and medical school. He has completed over 300 marathons and 70 ultramarathons, and after exhaustive research concluded that the best racing distance for him is 50 miles. Andy attributes his best runs to the camaraderie he shares while running with his friends and family. He takes pride in knowing he introduced his wife and children to running. His wife, Kathy, has completed 100 marathons, including one in each of the 50 states, and four of his children have two or more marathons under their belts. Andy has run every single Disney World Marathon and has his sights set on being in Orlando for its 25th anniversary in 2018. He has every intention of keeping his passion for running alive in the years ahead.

Marsha White—Marsha ran her first race, a half marathon, at the age of 59 and loved it. Since then she has completed over 200 marathons and ultramarathons in all 50 states, four Canadian provinces, and 10 countries. Now in her late 60s, she frequently places in her age group. Marsha has contributed articles about racing to several books and magazines, including a number of marathon reviews for *Marathon & Beyond*. When she's not traveling to races or writing about them, Marsha enjoys baking, sewing, reading, and quilting.

Amy Yanni—Amy, a self-proclaimed tomboy, has been running all of her life—from softball and tennis to her first race, a five-miler in Northampton, Massachusetts, just before the turn of the century. After being diagnosed with breast cancer in 2003, she started running marathons. Since that time, Amy has finished more than 140 marathons, including eight at Boston. She admits she runs a lot simply because she loves to run. Among her many credentials are sub 4-hour marathons in all 50 states after the age of 50 and running a brisk 1:36:03 half marathon at the age of 60 where she edged out Karin Miles, who competed in the Olympic Trials with Joanie Benoit.

Vikena Yutz—Vikena has been running since 2007, and it didn't take her long to fall in love with long-distance running. She ran her first ultramarathon in 2008 and has been hooked ever since. Her favorite ultra are the timed events where she has fared quite well over the years: 110 miles in 24 hours at Hinson Lake in Rockingham, North Carolina, and 254 miles in 72 hours and 367 miles in six days, both at Across the Years in Glendale, Arizona. In her short tenure in the sport, she has set several course records and hopes to set a few more in the years ahead.

RUNNING TO **EXTREMES**

EPILOGUE

You've met some amazing athletes in the pages of this book. One you haven't met is Darryl Beardall. What he lacks in words he more than makes up for in miles. Our staff statistician Craig Snapp writes:

Darryl Beardall has a lifetime mileage total of over 287,000 miles, which is more than anyone else on earth. In fact, that mileage could stretch from the earth to the moon (and one-fifth of the way back). Michael Jackson had his moonwalk, while Darryl Beardall has his moonrun.

And it's not like he's done these miles in the vacuum of space. For lack of a better term, he's a "serial racer." I know folks who have done 57 races. However, Darryl has done the Annual Dipsea Race 57 times! (It's a handicapped race in which everyone's starting time is based on their expected finish time, and the first to cross the finish line might not be the fastest, yet is declared the winner). He was the fastest in 1961 and 1963, and the winner in 1974 and 1978! He's done the Deseret News Marathon (one of his total of over 250 Marathons) 42 times and the Napa Valley Marathon 34 times. His lifetime race total is over 1,600 miles. Be sure to keep in mind those were in the days when there weren't a dozen races within driving distance every single weekend. At his peak, he competed in four Olympic Trials, with two eighth-place finishes and one ninth-place finish.

And, it's not like he's done these races at a slogger's pace. Here are some of his PRs:

- 100 miles 12:30 7:30 per mile
- 50 miles 5:18 6:22 per mile
- Marathon 2:28 5:40 per mile
- 10K 29:50 4:48 per mile
- 5K 14:45 4:44 per mile

He started his accumulation of astronomical mileage on the first of February 1954 and, for the next five years, averaged 40 miles per week. In 1959, he turned it up a notch—a BIG notch. For the next 36 years, he averaged over 120 miles per week. That would be over 17 miles per day, if one ran seven days per week. However, as Darryl is a Mormon and does not do any training runs on Sundays, he actually averaged over 20 miles per day. Whichever daily average one wishes to choose, the period involved accounts for more than 13,000 days. The next four years, he averaged 70 per week, the next nine, 100 per week, and the next four, back to 70. For the last two years, he's averaged just under 60 miles a week.

This book has chronicled the lives and accomplishments of 15 amazing runners—and equally amazing human beings. Each and every one of them—Ray, Mike, Amy, Dean, Mark, Mike, Bobbi, Marshall, Pam, Larry, Tim, Ed, Eric, Ann, and Helen—continue their torrid love affairs to this day with the greatest sport on the planet: running. Some of them may not run as far as they used to run, and many of them not as fast, but all of them run with the same passion and appreciation they had on the day they laced up their first pair of running shoes.

Speaking for all of the runners who were portrayed in this book, the runners who authored this book, and the runners who were responsible

RUNNING TO **EXTREMES**

for the introductions in this book, it is our hope that you have gained some insight into realizing that everyone is capable of accomplishing great things if the right amount of blood, sweat, tears, and, most of all, *heart* is put into it.

Finally, all of us share a mutual respect for the many runners the world over who continue doing amazing things in their own right—each and every day.

Now if you'll excuse us, we're going out for a run.

Care to join us?

ACKNOWLEDGEMENTS

The back cover photo of Ted Corbitt was taken by Peter Roth and generously donated by his son, Gary Corbitt.

The photograph of Marshall Ulrich and Scott Ludwig was staged and taken by their better halves: Heather and Cindy, respectively.

The photograph of Marshall Ulrich is courtesy of Brett Hochmuth of Eagle Eye Photography.

The photograph of Ann Trason is courtesy of Martin Jones.

The photograph of Ray Zahab is courtesy of Jon Golden.

The photograph of Eric Clifton is courtesy of Ben Jones.

The photograph of Tim Twietmeyer and his son, Austin, are courtesy of Joe McCladdie.

The photographs of all of the other athletes are from their respective personal collections.

My sincerest thanks to the many people who lent a hand in assembling this book:

Susanne Thurman, for preparing the photographs and answering my plethora of questions about formatting and layout (no easy task).

RUNNING TO EXTREMES

Janeshia Neeley, for meticulously transcribing all of the recorded telephone interviews Scott Ludwig conducted with his subjects.

The various contributors who wrote such eloquent, heart-felt introductions to the chapters.

The special athletes who volunteered to bare their souls (as well as their soles) and allowed their stories to be told in these pages.

The handful of authors who did the telling. Ya'll done good. Very, very good.

It's been a long time coming for this book to see the light of day. It has been my extreme honor and privilege to have had the opportunity to work with the amazing people who have helped make this book possible.

From all of us, we hope you enjoyed it.

If so, be sure to spread the word.

Ideally while you're out running on the roads or trails.

APPENDICES

RAY ZAHAB—RUNNING AND EXPEDITION CAREER HIGHLIGHTS

May 2014	i2P Youth Expedition Atacama youth project.
March 2014	Completed fourth crossing of Baffin Island
December 2013	i2P Youth Expedition Peru youth project
Summer 2013	Ran 2,000-plus kilometers (1,243 miles) across Mongolia and the Gobi Desert
May 2013	i2P Youth Expedition Utah youth project
November 2012	i2P Expedition Botswana youth project
September 2012	Ran nonstop with Ferg Hawke across Baffin Island (training run for upcoming 2,300 kilometer [1,429 miles] crossing of the Gobi Desert)
November 2012	i2P Expedition Botswana youth project
September 2012	Ran nonstop with Ferg Hawke across Baffin Island (training run for upcoming 2,300 kilometer [1,429 miles] crossing of the Gobi Desert)
December 2011	i2P Expedition India youth project
August 2011	Ran approximately 240 kilometers (149 miles) from north park boundary to south park boundary of Death Valley (completely off road)
May 2011	i2P Expedition Bolivia youth project
January 2011	Ran length of Atacama Desert (1,191 kilometers [740 miles] from Peruvian border to Copiapo, Chile, in 20 days)

RUNNING TO EXTREMES

October 2010	i2P Expedition Amazon youth project
May 2010	i2P Running Tunisia youth project
February 2010	Ran 650 kilometers (404 miles) in 13 days (unsupported) across Lake Baikal in Siberian winter
September 2009	i2P Expedition Baffin youth project
January 2009	Trekked 1,200 kilometers (746 miles; unsupported) as member of three-man team to Geographic South Pole from Hercules Inlet (33 days, 23 hours, 55 minutes)
May 2008	Ran an average of 80 kilometers (50 miles) a day in each of Canada's 13 provinces and territories in 13 days
August 2007	Ran three coastal trails of Canada (Akshayuk Pass, Baffin/East Coast Trail/West Coast Trail) back to back in eight days
November 2006	Ran 7,500 kilometers (4,660 miles) from Senegal to Red Sea, crossing the Sahara Desert in 111 days
May 2006	Completed Gobi March, 250-kilometer (155 miles) race organized by RacingThePlanet; was on the first-place team
February 2006	Earned first place in Libyan Challenge, 190 kilometers (118 miles) nonstop
October 2005	Earned first place in Sahara Race, 250-kilometer (155 miles) race organized by RacingThePlanet
April 2004, 2005	Marathon Des Sables, 243 kilometers (151 miles)
November 2004	Ran Trans 333 Niger, 333 kilometers (207 miles) nonstop, earning third place

APPENDICES

October 2004	Ran Jungle Marathon Amazon, 200 kilometers (124 miles), earning eight place solo and first place team
February 2004	Ran Yukon Arctic Ultra, 150 kilometers (93 miles) nonstop, earning first place

RUNNING TO EXTREMES

DEAN KARNAZES—AN AMAZING, DIVERSE CAREER

TIME magazine named him one of the "Top 100 Most Influential People in the World." *Men's Fitness* hailed him as one of the fittest men on the planet. Stan Lee called him, "Super Human." An acclaimed endurance athlete and *NY Times* bestselling author, Dean Karnazes has pushed his body and mind to inconceivable limits. Among his many accomplishments, he has run 350 continuous miles, foregoing sleep for three nights. He's run across the Sahara Desert in 120-degree Fahrenheit temperatures, and he's run a marathon to the South Pole in negative 40 degrees Fahrenheit. On 10 different occasions he's run a 200-mile relay race solo, racing alongside teams of 12. Dean has swum the San Francisco Bay, has scaled mountains, has bike raced for 24-hours straight, and has surfed the gigantic waves off the coast of Hawaii. His long list of competitive achievements include winning the world's toughest footrace, the Badwater Ultramarathon, running 135 miles nonstop across Death Valley during the middle of summer. He has raced and competed on all seven continents of the planet, twice over.

In 2006, he accomplished the seemingly impossible by running 50 marathons in all 50 US states in 50 consecutive days, finishing with the NYC Marathon, which he ran in three hours flat! In 2011, Dean ran 3,000 miles from the coast of California to New York City, averaging 40 to 50 miles per day (one day covering more than 70). Along the way, he stopped at schools to speak to students about the importance of exercise and healthy eating. When passing through Washington, D.C., he was invited to run through the White House to meet with First Lady Michelle Obama and be honored for his tireless commitment to help get this country back into shape.

Dean and his incredible adventures have been featured on *The Today Show, 60 Minutes, The Late Show with David Letterman, CBS News,*

APPENDICES

CNN, ESPN, The Howard Stern Show, Morning Edition: NPR, Late Night with Conan O'Brien, the BBC, and many others. He has appeared on the cover of *Runner's World, Outside*, and *Wired* magazines and has been featured in *TIME, Newsweek, People, GQ, The New York Times, USA TODAY, Washington Post, Men's Journal, Forbes, Chicago Tribune, Los Angeles Times*, and the *London Telegraph*, to mention a few. Dean is the winner of an *ESPN* ESPY and a three-time recipient of *Competitor* magazine's Endurance Athlete of the Year award.

Yet, it is his unique ability to enthuse athletes of all abilities and backgrounds that truly sets Dean apart. Despite his many accomplishments, awards, and distinctions, he remains most proud of his ongoing contributions of time and funding to programs aimed at getting children and youth outdoors and active. He has raised millions of dollars for charity and was awarded the prestigious Community Leadership Award by the President's Council on Fitness, Sports & Nutrition.

Beyond being a celebrated endurance athlete, philanthropist, and bestselling author, Dean is an accomplished businessman with a notable professional career working for several Fortune 500 companies and startups, alike. A graduate of the USF McLaren School of Business & Management, he is uniquely able to demonstrate how the lessons learned from athletics can be applied to business, and he is able to convey, with authenticity, the many insights he has gleaned along the way as a record-setting athlete and professional businessman.

Dean is a sought-after speaker who has captivated and inspired audiences across the globe with his stories of persistence and perseverance. His dynamic, engaging, and rousing presentations focus on going beyond perceived limitations to be the best that you can be. He talks about unlocking an inner strength to achieve extraordinary results. His real-life examples explore these topics: dealing with adversity, overcoming

RUNNING TO EXTREMES

obstacles, setting and reaching lofty goals, understanding the importance of teamwork—even in solo endeavors, and excelling in a competitive and often confusing world. In his presentations, he examines and discusses the essential ingredients necessary for high achievement and developing the ability to prevail and persevere against staggering odds.

Dean is believable because his achievements and accomplishments are real. He delivers his message with the insight and candor that only an individual who has lived through such experiences can. Dean's stories of endurance and perseverance are often comical, sometimes tear jerking, and always thought-provoking and entertaining. His roster of clients include: Nike, Google, Sony, PepsiCo, Wells Fargo, Apple Computer, Merck, Toyota, Starbucks, Accenture, Stanford University, Yale, JPMorgan Chase, Amazon, Facebook, and a host of others.

MARSHALL ULRICH—CAREER HIGHLIGHTS

Qualifications

- The only person in the world to complete the *triple crown of extreme sports*: world-class ultrarunner, record setting adventure racer, and Seven Summits mountaineer.
- Completed over 127 ultra and adventure races, averaging over 125 miles each; multiple record holder.
- Grand masters record holder for running across the United States (and beat the masters record).
- One of three people in the world to have competed in all nine Eco Challenge adventure races and has competed in 16 expedition-length adventure races with 12 ranked finishes.
- Reached the summit of each of the Seven Summits, including Mount Everest, all on first attempts.
- Raised over $850,000 for numerous charities, including the Religious Teachers Filippini.
- Experienced public speaker, including business-oriented, motivational, technical training, and entertaining presentations for businesses, universities, sports teams, and professional conferences.

RUNNING TO EXTREMES

Ultrarunning—
World Class Distances and Multiple Record Holder

Record Holder	Grand masters and third fastest ever, running 3,063 miles (equivalent to 117 marathons) across the U.S.—San Francisco to New York City in 52 days, 11 hours, and 58 minutes
Joint Record Holder	First-ever self-supported, 425-mile circumnavigation of Death Valley National Park (along with Dave Heckman), completed in July/August in just over 16 days
Record Holder	Running across Death Valley from Badwater (minus 282 feet) to the top of Mount Whitney (14,496 feet), covering 146 miles in 33 hours and 54 minutes
Record Holder	Four-time winner of Badwater 135 desert race—former record 26 hours and 18 minutes
Record Holder	19-time finisher of Badwater 146 and a record 26 crossings of Death Valley
Record Holder	133 miles south to north crossing of Death Valley Monument in 28 hours and 01 minute
Former Record Holder	First person to finish a self-contained, unaided, solo run pulling a 220-pound cart 146 miles from Badwater to the top of Mount Whitney in 77 hours and 46 minutes
Record Holder	First person to complete Badwater Quad—584 miles from Badwater to the top of Mount Whitney and back again, twice, in 10.5 days
Record Holder	258-mile Run Across Ohio in 64 hours and 09 minutes

APPENDICES

Record Holder	Three-time winner of 310-mile Run Across Colorado in 88 hours and 14 minutes
Former Record Holder	First person to complete the Death Valley Cup, finishing the Badwater Ultra plus the Furnace Creek 508 in the same summer in 71 hours and 32 minutes
Record Holder	Only person to ever complete the Leadville Trail 100 Run/Pikes Peak Marathon combination on the same weekend; total elapsed time, 36 hours and 34 minutes
Record Holder	Only person to complete the Leadville Triple Crown—Leadville 100-mile bike, 100-mile run, and 100-mile kayak on consecutive weekends
Former Record Holder	First person to complete all six American 100-mile trail runs in one year
Silver Medalist	24-hour National Championships 1988, 1990; over 133 and 142 miles, respectively
Former Record Holder	1992 and 1993 Colorado 24-hour champion and record holder
Thirteen Leadville Trail 100 Finishes	Four top-10 finishes and seven sub-24-hour buckles
Five Western States Finishes	All five sub-24-hour buckles
Fourth Place American	Marathon Des Sables, Africa
Sixth Place	Iditafoot 100-mile footrace, Alaska

RUNNING TO EXTREMES

4 Deserts Races	Sahara Race 2005 in Egypt, earning 28th place; Gobi March in 2007, China, earning third place team
Personal Bests	48 hours, 202 miles; 24 hours, 142 miles; 15:28, 100 miles; and 6:19, 50 miles

Adventure Racing—Record All nine Eco Challenges

2003 Primal Quest	16th place U.S. team, 23rd place overall, California
2002 Eco Challenge	8th place U.S. team, 17th place overall (23 of 81 teams finished), Fiji
2002 Raid Gauloises	Participant, Vietnam
2001 Eco Challenge	6th place U.S. team, 18th place overall, New Zealand
2001 Expedition BVI	Finisher, Team DuPont Challenged Athlete, British Virgin Islands
2000 Eco Challenge	4th place U.S. team, 12th place overall, Sabah/Borneo
2000 Raid Gauloises	Highest all U.S. team finish, 7th place overall, Tibet and Nepal
2000 Adrenaline Rush	All-male three-man team 1st place, 2nd place overall, Ireland
1999 Eco Challenge	6th place U.S. team, 19th place overall, Patagonia, Argentina
1998 Eco Challenge	4th place U.S. team, 10th place overall, Morocco

APPENDICES

1997 Eco Challenge	26th place overall, Australia
1997 Raid Gauloises	1st place all U.S. team, 13th place overall, South Africa
1996 Eco Challenge	Participant, Canada
1996 Extreme Games	Participant, Mexico
1995 Eco Challenge/ESPN Extreme Games	1st place U.S. team, 2nd place overall, Maine
1995 Eco Challenge	Unranked finisher, Utah

Mountaineering—The Seven Summits

Mount Everest	29,035 feet, highest point in Asia and the world, May 25, 2004, north side, Tibet
Aconcagua	22,840 feet, highest point in South America, February 1, 2003, Argentina
Denali	20,320 feet, highest point in North America, June 16, 2002, Alaska
Kilimanjaro	19,340 feet, highest point in Africa, July 2, 2003, Tanzania (again in 2006)
Mount Elbrus	18,481 feet, highest point in Europe, June 14, 2004, Russia
Mount Vinson	16,067 feet, highest point in Antarctica, January 12, 2005, Antarctica

RUNNING TO **EXTREMES**

Mount Kosciusko	7,310 feet, highest point in Australia, March 10, 2005, Australia
Mount Blanc	15,774 feet, highest point in western Europe, July 9, 2006, France
Mexican Volcanoes	Orizaba, Ixta, and Toluca, guided trips October 2004, 2005, and 2006, Mexico
Ecuadorian Volcanoes and the Alps	Various technical peaks, Ecuador, Italy, France, Switzerland

Media and Publication Highlights

Author and documentary	*Running on Empty*, Avery/Penguin, April 2011; *Running America* documentary, April 2010
Television	AARP *My Generation*, *ABC's Wide World of Sports*, *Dateline NBC*, *Discovery*, *ESPN*, *HBO Real Sports*, *National Geographic*, *Outdoor Life Network*, *Real TV*, *Stan Lee's Superhumans*, the *Today Show*
Magazine	*AARP*, *Newsweek*, *Outside*, *Sports Illustrated*
Newspaper	Various
Author	Cover Sept/Oct 2006 *Marathon & Beyond* (*M&B*) with feature story "Transformation of an Adventure Runner…From the Farm to Mount Everest…" by Marshall Ulrich
Contributing Author	*The Thrill of Victory, The Agony of My Feet*, ed. Neal Jamison, 2005, Breakaway Books
	Named top 10 "2004 Outdoor Person of the Year Award" by *Hooked on the Outdoors*, February 2005

APPENDICES

	Cover of June 2004 *Adventure Sports* and highlighted athlete "Over 50 and Kicking Your Butt"
Author	"When Out-and-Back Just Doesn't Get It Done: Badwater Quad," *M&B*, Jan/Feb 2004
	Named "Endurance King" by *Outside*, December 2001
	Cover of June/July 2001 *Trail Runner* and highlighted as one of the "Legends of the Trail"
Author	Cover of July/Aug 2000 M&B with feature story, "My Most Unforgettable Ultramarathon (And What I Learned From It): Death Valley 1999"

RUNNING TO **EXTREMES**

PAM REED—Running Career Highlights

Badwater Ultramarathon	Two-time champion and only woman to win, 2002 and 2003
Badwater Ultramarathon	40 to 49 age group record holder, 27:42:52, 2008 (bettered in 2015). Only woman to have 10 Badwater finishes
Completed	over 80 100-mile runs and over 100 ultramarathons
Qualified for Ironman® World Championships	2010 to 2013
Qualified for Ironman® 70.3® World Championships	2010 to 2014
24-Hour American women's record holder	138.96 miles, 2003
48-Hour American women's record holder	212 miles, 2004
Only woman to ever run 300 miles without stopping	2005
Self-Transcendence Six-Day Race	491 miles, 2009 (unofficial American record)

APPENDICES

2003 USA Track & Field Women's Ultra Runner of the Year	
2003 Competitor magazine Endurance Sports Athlete of the Year	
Gold Ironman All World Athlete	Top 1% of age group, 2013 to 2015
2015 Arrowhead 135	2nd place female (135-mile self-supported run in Minnesota in January)
2015 Western States, Hardrock and Badwater Ultramarathon	all completed within a six-week period.
Author	*The Extra Mile* (Rodale, 2006)
Race Director	Tucson Marathon, 1995 to present

RUNNING TO **EXTREMES**

HELEN KLEIN—RUNNING CAREER HIGHLIGHTS

Personal Data
Date of Birth: November 27, 1922
Wife, mother of four, grandmother of nine, great-grandmother of four, great-great-grandmother of two
Running career began—with no prior experience in 1978 at the age of 55
Holder of approximately 75 world and American running records
World Records
World's fastest times in her age group: 1 mile, 10 kilometers, marathon, 50 miles, 100 kilometers, 100 miles
World's longest distance in her age group: 24 hours (109.5 miles), 48 hours, 5 days, and 6 days (373 miles)
Notable Accomplishments
500-kilometer run across the state of Colorado in five days, 10 hours in 1991
90 marathon finishes
143 ultramarathon finishes (only one woman has more)
Oldest person to complete a 100-mile trail run
Official finisher of the Ironman Triathlon in Kona, Hawaii
Oldest woman to have finished the Western States Endurance Run, Leadville Trial 100 Run, Wasatch Front, Old Dominion, Angeles Crest, Rocky Raccoon, and Vermont (all 100-mile races)

At the age of...

66 became one of the first women to complete the grand slam of ultrarunning: 5 100-mile mountain trail runs (although only four are needed to constitute a slam) within a 16-week period, totaling 175,000 feet of elevation change
70 ran the 145-mile stage race in the Himalayas
72 completed the Marathon Des Sables, a 145-mile stage race across the Sahara Desert in Morocco; two weeks later completed the 370-mile Eco Challenge in Utah
74 ran the 143-mile stage race in the Peruvian Andes
80 broke the world record in the marathon by 39 minutes, running 4:31:32
81 completed the Tahoe Triple by running three marathons around Lake Tahoe on three consecutive days, 78.6 miles in 18:05:51
85 broke the world record in the marathon by 64 minutes, running 5:49:11; then three months later lowering it another 12 minutes, running 5:36:18

Coach (with husband Norm)

Team Diabetes Marathon Team	1999 to 2001
Barrett Middle School Track Team	2001 to 2007

RUNNING TO **EXTREMES**

Co-Race Director	
Western States Endurance Run	1986 to 1999
California International Marathon	1988 to 1992
Gibson Ranch Multi-Day Classic	1989 to 1995
Jed Smith Ultra Classic	1990 to 1994
Napa Valley Marathon	1992 to 1995
Sunmart Texas Trail 50-Mile/50K Run	1992 to 1999
Sedona-Pinewood 50-Mile Run	1993
Monument Valley 50-Mile Run	1995
Sierra Nevada Endurance 52.4-Mile Run	1999 to 2008
Helen Klein Ultra Distance Classic	1999 to 2010
Rio Del Lago 100-Mile Run	2000 to 2008
Awards and Honors	
MasterCard's Master of the Marathon Award—1992	
USA Track & Field Hall of Fame—First Woman Ultramarathoner (elected in 1999)	
Arete Award—Symbolizing Courage in Sports (ESPN)	
2002 Olympic Torch Bearer	
Road Runner's Hall of Fame—Elected in 2004	
Sacramento Running Association Hall of Fame—Elected in 2013	

ED ETTINGHAUSEN—2014 CHRONOLOGY OF EVENTS

01/11/2014	Enlightened Ultra 100	Long Beach	CA	29:56:00	100 mi
01/25/2014	Coldwater Rumble 100	Goodyear	AZ	31:37:53	100 mi
02/15/2014	Jackpot Ultra Running Festival 100	Las Vegas	NV	24:09:40	100 mi
03/01/2014	Razorback Endurance Race 125	San Martin	CA	29:43:59	125 mi
03/15/2014	Run 4 Kids 24-Hour Ultramarathon	Corona	CA	23:59:59	110.8 mi
03/21/2014	Antelope Island Buffalo Run 100	Syracuse	UT	26:48:04	100 mi
03/29/2014	Beyond Limits Ultra 24-Hour	Mountain Center	CA	23:38:59	108 mi
04/04/2014	Zion 100	Virgin	UT	33:57:13	100 mi
04/25/2014	Salt Flats 100	Wendover	UT	28:40:15	100 mi
05/03/2014	Nirvana 100	Big Bear	CA	29:21:00	100 mi
05/10/2014	Ride the Wind Trail Race 100	Las Vegas	NV	26:11:01	100 mi
05/17/2014	Born to Run 100	Los Olivos	CA	20:25:36	100 mi
05/24/2014	Nanny Goat 24-Hour	Riverside	CA	24:00:00	109 mi

RUNNING TO EXTREMES

05/31/2014	Santa Barbara (DRTE) 100	Santa Barbara	CA	29:34:48	100 mi
06/07/2014	San Diego 100	Lake Cayumaca	CA	26:46:40	100 mi
06/14/2014	Bryce 100	Bryce	UT	34:59:00	100 mi
06/21/2014	Summer Solstice 24-Hour Race	San Francisco	CA	23:50:32	115.7 mi
06/28/2014	Happy Jack 100	Laramie	WY	27:41:00	100 mi
07/04/2014	Merrill's Mile 24-Hour Race	Dahlonega	GA	24:00:00	104 mi
07/12/2014	Cool Your Ass 24-Hour Race	Prescott	AZ	24:00:00	104 mi
07/22/2014	Badwater 135	Lone Pine	CA	38:25:30	135 mi
08/04/2014	Six Days in the Dome	Anchorage	AK	144:00:00	415 mi
08/16/2014	Run-de-Vous 100	San Martin	CA	24:37:26	100 mi
08/26/2014	Silverton 6-Day	Silverton	CO	144:00:00	100 mi
08/29/2014	Silverton 72-Hour	Silverton	CO	72:00:00	101 mi
09/13/2014	Headlands 100	Sausalito	CA	31:12:11	100 mi
09/19/2014	Kodiak 100	Big Bear	CA		60 mi
09/26/2014	135M to the House	Bakersfield	CA	35:29:00	135 mi
10/11/2014	24 Hours of Boulder	Boulder	CA	23:59:59	100 mi
10/17/2014	Pony Express Trail 100	Faust	UT	21:45:57	100 mi

10/18/2014	Endurance Challenge 100	Norco	CA	29:09:00	101.6 mi
11/01/2014	Javelina Jundred	Fountain Hills	AZ	27:20:18	101.8 mi
11/08/2014	Rio Del Lago 100	Granite Bay	CA	28:43:06	100 mi
11/15/2014	Chimera 100	Cleveland National Forest	CA	30:41:27	100 mi
11/22/2014	Big Cedar Endurance Run 100	Dallas	TX	33:59:21	100 mi
11/29/2014	Soulmates Thanksgiving Tryptophun Rhuns 100	Waddell	AZ	26:52:10	100 mi
12/05/2014	Jester's World Record Run 24-Hour	Bonita	CA	23:50:00	103 mi
12/06/2014	Jester's World Record Run 100	Bonita	CA	35:58:00	100 mi
12/13/2014	Desert Solstice Track Invitational 24-Hour	Phoenix	AZ	24:00:00	114.9 mi
12/20/2014	Celtic Winter Classic 24-Hour	Bakersfield	CA	24:11:43	108 mi
12/28/2014	Across The Years 6-day	Glendale	AZ	144:00:00	414.2 mi

RUNNING TO **EXTREMES**

ANN TRASON—RUNNING CAREER HIGHLIGHTS

Western States Endurance Run	Fourteen-time women's winner; held course record (17:37) for 18 years until surpassed by Ellie Greenwood in 2012; 13 finishes in the top 10 overall
Leadville Trail 100	Four-time women's winner and course record holder (18:06); second overall in 1994; third overall in 1990
Grand Slam Finisher	79:23:21 in 1998, the fastest cumulative time by a female
Comrades Marathon (54 miles)	Two-time women's winner in 1996 and 1997; uphill women's course record holder, 6:13 set in 1996
100K World Championship	Two-time women's champion in 1995 and 1998; set world record 7:00:47 in 1995
1989 TAC 24-Hour National Championships	Only woman to win the National Track & Field Championships outright
Races won outright	Silver State 50-Mile Trail Run in 1994, Quicksilver 50-Mile Trail Run in 1992, Sri Chinmoy 100-Mile in 1991, Bay Area 12 Hour in 1989, and the 24-Hour National Championships 1989
U.S. Olympic Marathon Trials qualifier	Only person to qualify for the Olympic Marathon Trials while running a longer distance in 1988, 1992, and 1996

APPENDICES

Awards	1995 American Runner of the Year (*Runner's World* magazine); 1988 to 1998 and 2001 Ultra Runner of the Year (*Ultrarunning* magazine); 1998 to 1992, 1994 to 1995 USA Track & Field Ultra Runner of the Year; 1994 Hall of Fame inductee, Road Runners Club of America
Personal Bests– Road	40 miles, 4:26:13; 50 miles, 5:40:18; 100 miles, 13:47:31; 100K, 7:00:47; 12 hours, 90 miles
Personal Bests– Track	12 hours, 91 miles; 100 miles, 14:29:44; 100K, 7:48:14

TED CORBITT—CHRONOLOGY

Compiled by Gary Corbitt	
1919	Born January 31 in Dunbarton, South Carolina, to Alma Bing and John Henry Corbitt
1938	Graduated Woodward High School in Cincinnati, Ohio
1942	Graduated University of Cincinnati
1944	U.S. Army – World War II
1946	Married Ruth Eva Butler in Brooklyn, New York
1947	Joined the New York Pioneer Club
1949	Began a 44-year career at the International Center for the Disabled
1950	Earned a master's degree at New York University in Physical Therapy
1951	Ran his first marathon at Boston Son, Gary, was born
1952	Represented the U.S. Olympic Team in the marathon at Helsinki, Finland
1954	U.S. National Marathon Champion
1955	*Sports Illustrated* article
	Radio interview with Chris Schenkel
	Ebony magazine article
	Canadian National Marathon Champion
1956	Set an American record for the marathon on the track
	U.S. National Champion at 30 kilometers

APPENDICES

	Studied connective tissue massage from the originator of this technique, Elisabeth Dicke, in West Germany
1957	U.S. National Champion at 30 Kilometers
1958	First president of the New York Road Runners Club
	Started a quarterly, *New York Road Runners Newsletter*; served as editor for 20 years
	Personal best marathon time set in Philadelphia: 2:26:44
	Finished an unofficial sixth place at the Boston Marathon after failing the pre-race physical; Al Confalone and John Lafferty also failed the pre-race physical
	Began teaching at Columbia University
1959	Won the first ultramarathon conducted by the New York Road Runners Club; the distance was 30 miles, which he ran in 3:04:13
1960	Became the third national president of Road Runners Club of America
	Co-authored a pioneering textbook on hydrotherapy with Gertrude Finnerty
	Started the National Road Runners Club Newsletter now called *Club Running*
	Studied PNF (proprioceptive neuromuscular facilitation) stretching with Margaret Knott at Boston University
1962	Made the first of five trips overseas to run London-to-Brighton 52.5-mile road race

255

RUNNING TO **EXTREMES**

	Set a U.S. road and newcomer record with a fourth-place finish
1963	National RRC Ultramarathon 44-Mile Champion
1964	Wrote and published a monograph called *Measurement of Road Running Courses*
	Second-place finish at London-to-Brighton 52.5-mile race; set U.S. road record
1965	First chairman of the National Standards Committee which certified accurate distances of road race courses.
	Second-place finish at London-to-Brighton 52.5-mile race
1966	Ran 312.5 training miles in 7 days—during a workweek
	Set U.S. record for 50 miles on the track
	Fifth-place finish at London-to-Brighton 52.5-mile race
	Became the second runner in history to finish 100 marathons
1968	13-year streak of running two workouts per day ended
	U.S. National 50-Mile Champion
1969	Completed 132nd marathon to surpass Mike O'Hara
	Begins a 12-year period of having run more marathons than anyone in the history of the sport

256

APPENDICES

	Ran 1,002 training miles in July
	Set U.S. record for 100 miles on the track
1970	Second-place finish at London-to-Brighton 52.5-mile race; set U.S. and masters road record
	At age 51, set an American age group record for 50 miles on the road of 5:34:01; the record still stands today, over 45 years later
1971	Inducted to Road Runners Club of America Hall of Fame
1972	Tied the record of Clarence DeMar for most consecutive Boston Marathons run under three hours (19 times) from 1954 to 1972
	Studied PNF (proprioceptive neuromuscular facilitation) stretching with Dorothy Voss at Northwestern University
1973	Ran 207.2 training miles during a five-day workweek, averaging 41.4 miles per day
	Ran 50-mile training runs (three workouts) on a workday
	Set U.S. record for 24 hours on the track
1974	Subject of a biography, *Corbitt*, by John Chodes
1975	Suggested the concept of a Five Borough race to celebrate the Bicentennial; this became the Five Borough New York City Marathon
1981	Inducted to University of Cincinnati Athletic Hall of Fame
1993	Retired from the International Center for the Disabled

	Continued to treat patients until September 2007
1998	Inducted in the inaugural class National Distance Running Hall of Fame
2001	Set a world age record 303 miles in a six-day race at age 82
2003	Walked 68.7 miles in 24 hours; the race celebrated the 30th anniversary of his American record; this was Ted Corbitt's 223rd and last marathon and ultramarathon
2004	Journeyed to Athens, Greece, to see the birthplace of the Olympic Games
2005	Returned to Helsinki, Finland, to attend the World Track & Field Championships
2007	Lifetime Achievement Award *Runner's World* Heroes of Running

Life is the ultimate marathon; stay on the course and stay strong.

On December 12, 2007, Ted Corbitt passed away.

His legacy, however lives on…

CREDITS:

Photos: p.128, imago-sportfotodienst
　　　　all other photos, see p.229

Cover design: Sannah Inderelst

Cover graphic: ©Thinkstockphotos/iStock

Layout & typesetting: Sannah Inderelst

Copyediting: Elizabeth Evans

Subscribe to our newsletter at **www.m-m-sports.com**

OTHER BOOKS BY SCOTT LUDWIG

Scott Ludwig
RUNNING ULTRAS
TO THE EDGE OF EXHAUSTION

352 p., b/w,
23 photos,
Paperback 5 1/2" x 8 1/2"

ISBN: 9781782550464

$ 14.95 US/$ 22.95 AUS
£ 9.95 UK/€ 14.95

Scott Ludwig
A FEW DEGREES FROM HELL
WHITE HOT TALES FROM THE BADWATER ULTRAMARATHON

208 p., b/w,
31 photos, 3 illus.,
Paperback 6 1/2" x 9 1/4"

ISBN: 9781782550037

$ 16.95 US/$ 29.95 AUS
£ 12.95 UK/€ 16.95

All information subject to change © Thinkstock/iStockphoto

YOUR JOURNEY TO MINDFUL AND PASSIONATE RUNNING

c. 304 p., b/w,
c. 30 photos + illus.
Paperback, 5 1/2" x 8 1/2"

ISBN: 9781782550754

c. $ 14.95 US/$ 22.95 AUS
£ 9.95 UK/€ 13.95

Gary Dudney
THE TAO OF RUNNING
THE JOURNEY TO MINDFUL AND PASSIONATE RUNNING

The Tao of Running offers a fresh perspective on the mental side of running while entertaining with vivid tales of running adventures.

Going well beyond the standard training and racing advice found in most running books, it guides runners to a wider understanding of how running fits into their own aspirations, goals, and life philosophy.

MEYER & MEYER Sport
Von-Coels-Str. 390
52080 Aachen
Germany

Phone +49 02 41 - 9 58 10 - 13
Fax +49 02 41 - 9 58 10 - 10
E-Mail sales@m-m-sports.com
E-Books www.m-m-sports.com

All books available as E-books.

MEYER & MEYER SPORT

Subscribe to our newsletter at **www.m-m-sports.com**

NEVER GIVE UP!

Fiona Ford
BACK ON TRACK
HOW I RECOVERED FROM A LIFE-CHANGING ACCIDENT AND GOT BACK ON THE PODIUM

This book tells the story of former Pro triathlon athlete Fiona Ford's rehabilitation and recovery from a serious bike accident that ended her competitive career. It also provides practical guidance with advice, sessions and experiences from athletes who have successfully used sport for rehabilitation back to competitive form.

280 p., in color,
88 photos, 37 illus.,
Paperback 5 3/4" x 8 1/2"

ISBN: 9781782550747

$ 16.95 US/$ 23.95 AUS
£ 11.95 UK/€ 14.95

All information subject to change © Thinkstock/iStockphoto

MEYER & MEYER Sport
Von-Coels-Str. 390
52080 Aachen
Germany

Phone +49 02 41 - 9 58 10 - 13
Fax +49 02 41 - 9 58 10 - 10
E-Mail sales@m-m-sports.com
E-Books www.m-m-sports.com

All books available as E-books.

MEYER & MEYER SPORT